THE
DELL BOOK
OF
LOGIC
PROBLEMS #2

THE
DELL BOOK
OF
LOGIC
PROBLEMS #2

Editor-in-Chief • Rosalind Moore

Executive Editor • Erica L. Rothstein

Special Editor • Kathleen Reineke

A Dell Trade Paperback

A DELL TRADE PAPERBACK
Published by
Dell Publishing
a division of
Bantam Doubleday Dell Publishing Group, Inc.
1540 Broadway
New York, NY 10036

ISBN: 0-440-51875-X

Printed in the United States of America

November 1986

20 19 18 17 16
KPP

A WORD ABOUT THIS BOOK

Why do Logic Problems have such widespread popularity? Why do they appeal to solvers of all skill levels—of all ages—in all walks of life? Perhaps it's because they don't require an extensive vocabulary or a great store of knowledge to solve. Everyone starts out, more or less, on the same footing. Any information you need to solve a Logic Problem is always given in the clues. All you have to do is piece it together to arrive at the correct solution. So, Logic Problems pose the same challenge for everyone. It may not be the challenge of climbing a mountain that no one else has ever climbed; or the challenge of winning your first marathon, or just finishing one; but a challenge nonetheless—the challenge of a job well done. Some of you may already know the feeling of accomplishment you get when you have successfully completed a particularly complicated problem, but for those of you who are new to Logic Problems, take our word for it—the exhilaration might even be comparable to that mountain climber's or that marathon runner's. But we'll leave the comparisons and accomplishments up to you.

With this Introduction we welcome you to The Dell Book of Logic Problems #2. Like its predecessor, this book contains seventy-five never-before-published puzzles created just for you by the world's top Logic Problem constructors. These same constructors have been creating their logical masterpieces for the extensive line of Dell puzzle publications for over two decades. During that time Logic Problems have become one of the most popular forms of puzzle entertainment. To satisfy the demand we created this book devoted entirely to Logic Problems.

We hope you enjoy this assortment of all-new Logic Problems, each of which has been lovingly chosen, trial-solved, edited, and assembled here to bring you endless hours of stimulating entertainment. All comments, both pro and con, regarding this book are welcomed. Write to:

THE EDITORS
Dell Puzzle Publications
Dell Publishing
a division of
The Bantam Doubleday Dell
Publishing Group, Inc.
1540 Broadway
New York, New York 10036

Dear Logic Problem fans:

There are more of you than ever was expected! When the first *Dell Book of Logic Problems* became available, great numbers of you ran to your bookstores and went home happily with your copies; then you wrote to us. We received many, many letters, mostly saying the same thing: The book was a delight and when is the next one coming out? How about monthly? How about more Logics in the Dell puzzle publications? We got to work immediately and now number two in this peerless series is in your hands. Now you can look forward to these 75 brand new Logic Problems, representing the best Logics by the best constructors in the world of puzzles.

This book was not created by one person alone; it represents the combined efforts of all the Dell puzzle editors, who worked with constructors, and who trial-solved and rewrote and did all the things that editors are supposed to do to make the Logic Problems better, or clearer, or more fun.

If you enjoy this book, or want to make a comment, we would love to hear from you. A letter to the address given below will arrive at the right place, and whatever you have to say will be considered with an open mind and the sincere desire to listen.

Our thanks to all who make these books possible, but most of all, thanks to you, the Logic fan, for wanting more!

Sincerely,
Rosalind Moore
Editor-in-Chief
DELL PUZZLE PUBLICATIONS
1540 Broadway
New York, New York 10036

CONTENTS

EASY LOGIC PROBLEMS

MEDIUM LOGIC PROBLEMS

HARD LOGIC PROBLEMS

CHALLENGER LOGIC PROBLEMS

THE
DELL BOOK
OF
LOGIC
PROBLEMS #2

HOW TO SOLVE LOGIC PROBLEMS

For those of you who are new to Logic Problems: On the following pages you will find some insights into the thought processes that go into solving these puzzles, as well as detailed instructions on the use of charts as solving aids. We suggest you scan these instructions to familiarize yourself with the techniques presented here. Whenever you feel that you're ready to try your hand at solving, turn to the first puzzle (which you will find on page 27) and dig right in. If, even after you have studied these instructions, you should find yourself stuck while solving, turn to the solution for that puzzle and try to follow the reasoning given there. The solutions are not just a listing of "who did what," but rather a step-by-step elimination of possibilities, which you should find invaluable on your journey along the road to mastery of Logic Problems.

The 75 Logic Problems in this book are just that—problems based on logic, to which you need bring no specialized knowledge or extensive vocabulary. Instead, all you will need is your common sense, some reasoning power, and a basic grasp of how to use the charts or other solving aids provided. The problems themselves are all classic deduction problems, in which you are usually asked to figure out how two or more sets of facts relate to each other—what first name belongs with which last name, for example. All of the facts you will need to solve each puzzle are always given.

The puzzles are mostly arranged in increasing order of difficulty—the first few are rather easy to solve, then the puzzles get more difficult as you continue through the book. The final puzzles are especially challenging. If you are new to Logic Problems, we suggest that you start with the first puzzles, progressing through the book as you get more expert at solving.

Of the three examples which follow, the first is, of course, the most basic, but the skills utilized there will help you tackle even the most challenging challenger. Example #2 will help you hone those skills and gives valuable hints about the use of a more complicated chart as a solving aid. The third member of the group will introduce those puzzles for which the normal solving chart is not applicable. You will notice that in each of these examples, as in all the Logic Problems in this book, the last part of the introduction will tell you what facts you are to establish in solving that puzzle. Now, if you are ready to begin, read through the introduction and the clues given with Example #1.

15

EXAMPLE #1

A young woman attending a party was introduced to four men in rather rapid succession and, as usual at such gatherings, their respective types of work were mentioned rather early in the conversation. Unfortunately, she was afflicted with a somewhat faulty memory. Half an hour later, she could remember only that she had met a Mr. Brown, a Mr. White, a Mr. Black, and a Mr. Green. She recalled that among them were a photographer, a grocer, a banker, and a singer, but she could not recall which was which. Her hostess, a fun-loving friend, refused to refresh her memory, but offered four clues. Happily, the young woman's logic was better than her memory, and she quickly paired each man with his profession. Can you? Here are the clues:

1. Mr. White approached the banker for a loan.

2. Mr. Brown had met the photographer when he hired him to take pictures of his wedding.

3. The singer and Mr. White are friends, but have never had business dealings.

4. Neither Mr. Black nor the singer had ever met Mr. Green before that evening.

	Black	Brown	Green	White
banker				
grocer				
photo.				
singer				

You know from the last part of the introduction what it is you are to determine—you are to match each man's last name with his profession. The chart has been set up to help you keep track of the information as you discover it. We suggest that you use an X in a box to indicate a definite impossibility and a • (dot) in a box to show an established fact.

Your first step is to enter X's into the chart for all of the obvious possibilities that you can see from information given in the clues. It is apparent from clue 1 that Mr. White is not the banker, so an X would be entered into the White/banker box. Clue 2 makes it clear that Mr. Brown is not the photographer, so another X in the Brown/photographer box can be entered. Clue 3 tells you that Mr. White is not the singer. And from clue 4 you can see that neither Mr. Black nor Mr. Green is the singer. Each of these impossibilities should also be indicated by X's in the chart. Once you have done so, your chart will look like this:

	Black	Brown	Green	White
banker				X
grocer				
photo.		X		
singer	X		X	X

Remembering that each X indicates that something is *not* a fact, note the row of boxes at the bottom—corresponding to which of the men is the singer. There are four possibilities, and you have X's for three of them. Therefore, Mr. Brown, the only one left, has to be the singer. Put a dot (•) in the singer/Brown box. Also, remember that if Mr. Brown is the singer, he is not the photographer (which we knew, we have an X); and he cannot be the grocer or the banker either. Thus, you would put X's in those boxes too. Your chart would now look like this:

	Black	Brown	Green	White
banker		X		X
grocer		X		
photo.		X		
singer	X	•	X	X

Now you seem to have a "hopeless" situation! You have used all the clues, and you have matched one man with his profession—but the additional X's entered in the chart do not enable you to make another match, since the possibilities have not been narrowed down sufficiently. What to do next?

Your next step is to reread the clues, at the same time considering the new information you have acquired: You know that Mr. Brown is the singer and that he has done business with the photographer (clue 2). But the singer has never done business with Mr. White (clue 3) or with Mr. Green (clue 4). And that means that neither Mr. White nor Mr. Green can possibly be the photographer. You can now place X's in those boxes in the chart. After you have done so, here is what you will have:

	Black	Brown	Green	White
banker		X		X
grocer		X		
photo.		X	X	X
singer	X	•	X	X

And you see that you do have more answers! The photographer must be Mr. Black, since there are X's in the boxes for the other names. Mr. White, also, must be the grocer, since there is an X in the other three boxes under his name. Once you have placed a dot to indicate that Mr. Black is the photographer and a dot to show that Mr. White is the grocer (always remembering to place X's in the other boxes in the row and column that contain the dot) your chart will look like this:

	Black	Brown	Green	White
banker	X	X		X
grocer	X	X	X	•
photo.	•	X	X	X
singer	X	•	X	X

You can see that you are left with one empty box, and this box corresponds to the remaining piece of information you have not yet determined—what Mr. Green's profession is and who the banker is. Obviously, the only possibility is that Mr. Green is the banker. And the Logic Problem is solved!

Most of the Logic Problems in this book will ask you to determine how more than two sets of facts are related to each other. You'll see, however, that the way of solving a more involved Logic Problem is just the same as Example #1—*if* you have a grasp of how to make the best use of the solving chart. The next example of a Logic Problem is presented in order to explain how to use a bigger chart. As before, read through the problem quickly, noting that the introduction tells you what facts you are to determine.

17

EXAMPLE #2

Andy, Chris, Noel, Randy, and Steve—one of whose last name is Morse—were recently hired as refreshment vendors at Memorial Stadium; each boy sells only one kind of fare. From the clues below, try to determine each boy's full name and the type of refreshment he sells.

1. Randy, whose last name is not Wiley, does not sell popcorn.

2. The Davis boy does not sell soda or candy.

3. The five boys are Noel, Randy, the Smith boy, the Coble boy, and the boy who sells ice cream.

4. Andy's last name is not Wiley or Coble. Neither Andy nor Coble is the boy who sells candy.

5. Neither the peanut vendor nor the ice cream vendor is named Steve or Davis.

	Coble	Davis	Morse	Smith	Wiley	candy	ice.	pean.	pop.	soda
Andy										
Chris										
Noel										
Randy										
Steve										
candy										
ice.										
pean.										
pop.										
soda										

Note that the chart given is composed of three sets of boxes—one set corresponding to the first and last names; a second set (to the right) corresponding to first names and refreshment; and a third set, below the first set, corresponding to the refreshment and last names. Notice, too, that these sets are separated from each other by heavier lines so that it is easier to find the particular box you are looking for.

As in Example #1, your first step is to enter into the boxes of the chart the impossibilities. Keep in mind that you have many more boxes to be concerned with here. Remember, ROW indicates the boxes that go horizontally (the Andy row, for example) and the word COLUMN indicates the boxes that go vertically (the Coble column, for instance).

Clue 1 tells you that Randy's last name is not Wiley, and Randy does not sell popcorn. Thus, enter an X into the Randy/Wiley box and another X in the Randy/popcorn box in the Randy row. Clue 2 says that the Davis boy sells neither soda nor candy. Find Davis and go down that column to the Davis/soda box and put an X in it; then find the Davis/candy box in that same column and place an X in that box.

Clue 3 tells you a few things: It gives you all five of the boys, either by his first name (two of them), his last name (another two of them), or by what refreshment he sells (the remaining boy). You then know something about all five—one boy's first name is Noel, another's is Randy; a third boy has the last name Smith, a fourth has the last name Coble; and the fifth sells ice cream. All of these are different people. So, in the chart you have a lot of X's that can be entered. Noel's last name is neither Smith nor Coble, so enter X's in the Noel/Smith, Noel/Coble boxes; nor can Noel be the ice cream seller, so put an X in the Noel/ice cream box. Randy is neither Smith nor Coble, and Randy does not sell ice cream, so put the X's in the Randy/Smith, Randy/Coble, and Randy/ice cream boxes. And neither Smith nor Coble sells ice cream, so enter an X in those two boxes.

Clue 4 tells you that Andy's last name is neither Wiley nor Coble. It also says that Andy does not sell candy and neither does the Coble boy. By now you probably know where to put the X's—in the Andy/Wiley box, the Andy/Coble box, the Andy/candy box, and in the box in the Coble column corresponding to candy. From clue 5 you learn that neither Steve nor Davis is the boy who sells either peanuts or ice cream. (One important point here—read clue 5 again, and note that this clue does *not* tell you whether or not Steve's last name is Davis; it tells you only that neither the peanut seller nor the ice cream vendor has the first name Steve or the last name Davis.) Your chart should now look like this:

	Coble	Davis	Morse	Smith	Wiley	candy	ice.	pean.	pop.	soda
Andy	X				X	X				
Chris										
Noel	X			X			X			
Randy	X			X	X		X		X	
Steve							X	X		
candy	X	X								
ice.	X	X		X						
pean.		X								
pop.										
soda		X								

From this point on, we suggest that you fill in the above chart yourself as you read how the facts are established. If you look at the Davis column, you will see that you have X's in four of the refreshment boxes; the Davis boy is the one who sells popcorn. Put a dot in the Davis/popcorn box. Now, since it is Davis who sells popcorn, none of the other boys does, so you will put X's in all of the other boxes in that popcorn row.

Your next step will be to look up at the other set of refreshment boxes and see what first names already have an X in the popcorn column. Note that Randy has an X in the popcorn column (from clue 1). Thus, if you know that Randy does not sell popcorn, you now know that his last name is not Davis, since Davis is the popcorn seller. You can then put an X in the Randy/Davis box. After you've done this, you'll see that you now have four X's for Randy's last name. Randy has to be Morse, the only name left, so enter a dot in the Randy/Morse box. Don't forget, too, to enter X's in the boxes of the Morse column that correspond to the first names of the other boys.

Now that you know Randy is Morse, you are ready to look at what you've already discovered about Randy and transfer that information to the Morse column—remember that since Randy is Morse, anything that you know about Randy is also true of Morse, as they're the same person. You'll see that an X for Randy was entered from clue 3: Randy does not sell ice cream. Then Morse cannot be the ice cream seller either, so put an X in the Morse column to show that Morse doesn't sell ice cream.

Once the Morse/ice cream X is in place, note what you have established about the Wiley boy: His is the only last name left who can sell ice cream. Put the dot in the Wiley/ice cream box and enter X's in the Wiley column for all the other refreshments. Your next step? As before, you are ready to determine what this new dot will tell you, so you will go up to the other set of refreshment boxes and see what you have established about the ice cream vendor. He's not Noel or Steve—they have two X's already entered in the chart. Now that you have established the Wiley boy as the ice cream seller, you know that his first name can't be either Noel or Steve because neither of those boys sells ice cream. Once you've put X's in the Noel/Wiley box and the Steve/Wiley box, you'll see that you know who Wiley is. Remember that clue 4 had already told you that Andy's last name is not Wiley, so you have an X in the Andy/Wiley box. With the new X's, do you see that Wiley's first name has to be Chris? And since Chris is Wiley, and Wiley sells ice cream, so, of course, does Chris. Thus, you can put a dot in the Chris/ice cream box. And don't forget to put X's in the Chris row for the other refreshments and also in the ice cream column for the other first names.

Notice that once Chris Wiley is entered in the chart, there are now four X's in the Coble column, and Steve is the one who has to be the Coble boy. Put in the dot and then X's in the Steve row, and your chart looks like this:

	Coble	Davis	Morse	Smith	Wiley	candy	ice.	pean.	pop.	soda
Andy	X		X		X	X	X			
Chris	X	X	X	X	•	X	•	X	X	X
Noel	X		X	X	X		X			
Randy	X	X	•	X	X		X		X	
Steve	•	X	X	X	X		X	X		
candy	X	X			X					
ice.	X	X	X	X	•					
pean.		X			X					
pop.	X	•	X	X	X					
soda		X			X					

See that there are four X's in the Smith/first name column, so Smith's first name must be Andy. And Noel's last name is Davis, because he's the only one left. Remember— look down the Davis row and see—we already know Davis sells popcorn. So, Noel, whose last name is Davis, sells popcorn. And, of course, there should be X's in all the other boxes of the Noel row and the popcorn column.

Now that you have completely established two sets of facts—which first name goes with which last name—you can use the two sets of refreshment boxes almost as one. That is, since you know each boy's first name and last name, anything you have determined about a first name will hold true for that boy's last name; and, naturally, the reverse is true: whatever you know about a boy's last name must also be true of that boy's first name.

For example, you know that Coble is Steve, so look down the Coble column and note that you have already put X's in the candy, ice cream, and popcorn boxes. Go up to the Steve row and enter any X's that you know about Coble. After putting an X in the Steve/candy box, you'll see that you've determined that Steve sells soda. As always, don't forget to enter X's where appropriate once you've entered a dot to indicate a determined fact. These X's are what will narrow down the remaining possibilities.

Things are really moving fast now! Once you've entered the appropriate X's in the Steve row and the soda column, you will quickly see that there are four X's in the candy column—so, Randy (Morse) is the candy vendor. By elimination, Andy (Smith) sells peanuts and this Logic Problem is completely solved.

Many of the Logic Problems in this book will have charts that are set up much like the one in Example #2. They may be bigger, and the puzzle may involve matching more sets of facts, but the method of solving the Logic Problem using the chart will be exactly the same. Just remember:

Always read the whole problem through quickly. What you are to determine is usually stated in the last part of the introduction.

When using solving charts, use an X to indicate a definite impossibility and a • (dot) to indicate an established fact.

Once you have placed a dot to indicate an established fact, remember to put X's in the rest of the boxes in the row and the column that contains the dot.

Every time you establish a fact, it is a good idea to go back and reread the clues, keeping in mind the newly found information. Often, you will find that rereading the clues will help you if you seem to be "stuck." You may discover that you *do* know more facts than you thought you did.

Don't forget, when you establish a fact in one part of a solving chart, check to see if the new information is applicable to any other section of the solving chart—see if some X's or dots can be transferred from one section to another.

Just one other note before we get to Example #3, and this note applies to both the most inexperienced novice and the most experienced expert. If ever you find yourself stymied while solving a problem, don't get discouraged and give up—turn to the solution. Read the step-by-step elimination until you get to a fact that you have not established and see if you can follow the reasoning given. By going back and forth between the clue numbers cited in the solution and the clues themselves, you should be able to "get over the hump" and still have the satisfaction of completing the rest of the puzzle by yourself. Sometimes reading the solution of one puzzle will give you important clues (if you'll pardon the pun) to the thought processes involved with many other puzzles. And now to the last of our trio of examples.

Sometimes a Logic Problem has been created in such a way that the type of chart you learned about in Example #2 is not helpful in solving the problem. The puzzle itself is fine, but another kind of chart—a fill-in type—will better help you match up the facts and arrive at the correct solution. Example #3 is a puzzle using this type of solving chart.

EXAMPLE #3

It was her first visit home in ten years, and Louise wondered how she would manage to see her old friends and still take in the things she wanted to in the seven days she had to spend there. Her worry was needless, however, for when she got off the plane Sunday morning, there were her friends—Anna, Cora, Gert, Jane, Liz, and Mary—waiting to greet her with her seven-day visit all planned. The women knew that Louise wanted to revisit the restaurant where they always used to have lunch together, so Louise's vacation began that Sunday afternoon with a party. After that, each of the women had an entire day to spend with Louise, accompanying her to one of the following things: a ball game, concert, the theater, museum, zoo, and one day reserved for just shopping. From the clues below, find out who took Louise where and on what day.

1. Anna and the museum visitor and the woman whose day followed the zoo visitor were blondes; Gert and the concertgoer and the woman who spent Monday with Louise were brunettes. (*Note: All six women are mentioned in this clue.*)

2. Cora's day with Louise was not the visit that occurred the day immediately following Mary's day.

3. The six women visited with Louise in the following order: Jane was with Louise the day after the zoo visitor and four days before the museumgoer; Gert was with Louise the day after the theatergoer and the day before Mary.

4. Anna and the woman who took Louise shopping have the same color hair.

	Monday	Tuesday	Wednesday	Thursday	Friday	Saturday
friend						
activity						

As before (and always), read the entire puzzle through quickly. Note that here you are to determine which day, from Monday to Saturday, each woman spent with Louise and also what they did that day. The solving chart, often called a fill-in chart, is the best kind to use for this puzzle. You won't be entering X's and dots here; instead, you will be writing the facts into the chart as you determine them and also find out where they belong.

From clue 1 you can eliminate both Anna and Gert as the woman who took Louise to the museum and the concert. And neither of these activities took place on a Monday, nor did Anna or Gert spend Monday with Louise. You have discovered some things, but none of them can yet be entered into the chart. Most solvers find it useful to note these facts elsewhere, perhaps in the margin or on a piece of scratch paper, in their own particular kind of shorthand. Then when enough facts have been determined to begin writing them into the chart, you will already have them listed.

Do you see that clue 2 tells you Mary did not see Louise on Saturday? It's because the clue states that Cora's day was not the visit that occurred immediately following Mary's day, and thus, there had to be at least one visit after Mary's. You still don't have a definite fact to write into the chart. Don't lose heart, though, because . . .

. . . clue 3 will start to crack the puzzle! Note that this clue gives you the order of the six visits. Since the days were Monday through Saturday, the only possible way for Jane to be with Louise the day after the zoo visitor and four days before the museumgoer is if the zoo visit took place on Monday, Jane was with Louise on Tuesday, and the museumgoer was with Louise on Saturday. These facts can now be written into the chart—Monday zoo, Tuesday Jane, Saturday museum. Three days have been accounted for. The last part of clue 3 gives you the other three days: with

Wednesday, Thursday, and Friday still open, the theatergoer must be the Wednesday friend, Gert is the day after, or Thursday, and Mary saw Louise on Friday. These facts, too, should be written in the chart. Once you've done so, your chart will resemble this one:

	Monday	Tuesday	Wednesday	Thursday	Friday	Saturday
friend		Jane		Gert	Mary	
activity	zoo		theater			museum

Now go back to clue 1 and see what other facts you can establish. There are three blondes—Anna, the museum visitor, and the woman whose day followed the zoo visitor's. The chart shows you that this last woman was Jane. From clue 4 you learn that the woman who took Louise shopping and Anna have the same color hair—blond. The woman who took Louise shopping is not Anna (they're two separate people), nor is she the museum visitor, so she must be the woman whose day followed the zoo visitor's, Jane. That fact can be written in the chart.

You can also, at this point, establish what day Anna spent with Louise. Since you know it's not Monday (clue 1) and Anna is not the museumgoer (also clue 1), the only day left for her is Wednesday, so Anna took Louise to the theater. Clue 2 tells you that Cora's day did not immediately follow Mary's, so Cora's day can't be Saturday, and must be Monday. By elimination, Liz (listed in the introduction) spent Saturday with Louise at the museum.

It may be helpful to make a note of the hair colors mentioned in clue 1, perhaps under the relevant columns in the chart. These hair colors can again be used at this point. We've now established the blondes as Anna, Jane, and Liz; the brunettes are Gert, the concertgoer, and Cora. The only possibility is that Mary is the concertgoer. Everything has now been determined except what Gert did, so, by elimination, Gert must have taken Louise to a ball game (from the introduction).

	Monday	Tuesday	Wednesday	Thursday	Friday	Saturday
friend	Cora	Jane	Anna	Gert	Mary	Liz
activity	zoo	shopping	theater	ball game	concert	museum
	bru	blo	blo	bru	bru	blo

Are all Logic Problems easy to solve? No, of course not. Many of the puzzles in this book are much more complicated than the three examples and should take a great deal more time and thought before you arrive at the solution. However, the techniques you use to solve the puzzles are essentially the same. All the information needed to solve will be given in the puzzle itself, either in the introduction or the clues. As you eliminate possibilities, you will narrow down the choices until, finally, you can establish a certainty. That certainty will usually help narrow down the possibilities in another set of facts. Once you have determined something, you will probably need to return to the clues and reread them, keeping in mind what facts you have now established. Suddenly a sentence in the clues may well tell you something you could not have determined before, thus narrowing down the choices still further. Eventually you will have determined everything, and the Logic Problem will be solved.

EASY LOGIC PROBLEMS

1 CERAMICS PIECES

by Diane Yoko

Brenda and four of her friends who attended the same ceramics class, recently completed their masterpieces. Each made a different type of decorative piece; one made a statue that looked just like her pet poodle. From the clues that follow, can you determine the piece each made, and the order completed?

1. The fruit dish was completed after the ashtray but before Frieda's piece.

2. Caroline, who did not make the planter, was the first to finish.

3. Maxine finished her piece before both the ashtray, which was not Evelyn's project, and the candlesticks were completed.

The solution is on page 139.

The solution is on page 139.

	ashtray	candlesticks	fruit dish	planter	statue	1st	2nd	3rd	4th	5th
Brenda										
Caroline										
Evelyn										
Frieda										
Maxine										
1st										
2nd										
3rd										
4th										
5th										

2 THE MARATHON

by Margaret Shoop

1	In Hadensville last April 10,
2	They held their yearly race:
3	Twenty-six miles of sweat and pain,
4	Run at a grueling pace.
5	Who came in fifth? Who fourth? Who third?
6	Who was second and who the winner?
7	Here are the last names you must match:
8	Byrd, Jensen, Lane, North, and Zinner.
9	Match the last names with the first
10	(One runner's known as Lou),
11	And tell how each performed that day.
12	The clues below ensue.
13	The winner was a youngster;
14	Mr. Zinner's sixty-three.
15	Polly might have gotten fourth
16	If she hadn't bruised a knee.
17	Zinner didn't come in third.
18	Kenny's last name is Lane.
19	And Jensen won a higher place
20	In last year's race in rain.
21	The steepness of the final hill
22	Took its toll on many,
23	But, there, a spurt of energy
24	Pushed Michael on, past Kenny.
25	The latter came in second,
26	Way ahead of runner Byrd.
27	Byrd's first name isn't Joe,
28	The one who came in third.

The solution is on page 139.

	Byrd	Jensen	Lane	North	Zinner	1st	2nd	3rd	4th	5th
Joe										
Kenny										
Lou										
Michael										
Polly										
1st										
2nd										
3rd										
4th										
5th										

3 THE ACCOUNTING DEPARTMENT

by Lois Bohnsack

Four new accountants were hired recently by Global Consolidated. Each one worked in a different area of accounting: one worked in Accounts Receivable; one in Inventory; one in Internal Auditing; and one in Accounts Payable. From the clues below, determine each accountant's name and the area where she worked.

1. Ms. Taylor and the woman in Internal Auditing were sisters.

2. Brenda's last name was neither Stanley nor Taylor.

3. Dora's office was next door to Ms. Taylor's.

4. Ms. Reese and Anna were hired on Monday. The woman in Internal Auditing was hired on Tuesday.

5. Connie and the woman in Accounts Payable had lunch at 12 o'clock; Ms. Underwood and Brenda had lunch at 1 o'clock.

6. Dora does not work in Inventory or Internal Auditing.

The solution is on page 139.

The solution is on page 139.

	Reese	Stanley	Taylor	Underwood	Acc't Pay.	Acc't Rec.	Audit.	Inven.
Anna								
Brenda								
Connie								
Dora								
Acc't Pay.								
Acc't Rec.								
Audit.								
Inven.								

4 THRIFTY SHOPPERS

by W. H. Organ

Karen and four other young women who lived in the same building regularly shop at five different supermarkets. On one recent Saturday morning, each noticed advertised specials at a market at which one of the others shops and asked that neighbor to pick up two bargain items for her; one of the ten items was bacon. From the following clues, can you determine which market each woman patronizes, the two bargain items she purchased, and the neighbor for whom she bought them?

1. One of the women shops at the Four Star market, another at Foodland; neither is Louise.

2. Emily, who shops at Save More, purchased rice and one other item for her neighbor.

3. The woman who shops at Cost Less bought flour and pickles for Ellen.

4. Louise bought chicken and one other item for Betty, who does not shop at Foodland.

5. Emily asked Ellen to buy oranges and celery for her.

6. One of the women, who was not Louise, asked her neighbor to buy potatoes and corn for her.

7. The one who shops at Tip Top was not the one who bought hamburger for her neighbor.

The solution is on page 139.

Use the chart below to fill in the information as you discover it from reading the clues. You will find this kind of chart to be more helpful in solving this problem.

name	store	items bought		for whom

5 FOUR FENCES

by Ellen K. Rodehorst

Mr. Locke and three other men recently bought all four of the newly built houses on the north side of Lotus Lane. Each of the new owners, including Tom, began landscaping his backyard with the installation of a fence; all the fences are different designs. From the clues below, can you determine each man's full name, type of fence, and the location of his house on Lotus Lane?

1. A next-door neighbor of Ed installed a chain-link fence.

2. Mr. Post, who isn't the man with the picket fence, lives in the second house east of Joe's house.

3. A man who lives next door to Marvin built a horizontal board fence.

4. Mr. Key, who doesn't live next to Ed, admired the lattice fence that his next-door neighbor on the west built.

5. Marvin is not Mr. Gates.

6. Joe, who isn't the one with the lattice fence, does not live in the house at the west end of Lotus Lane.

The solution is on page 140.

We found this little map of the houses on Lotus Lane to be more helpful than the usual solving chart.

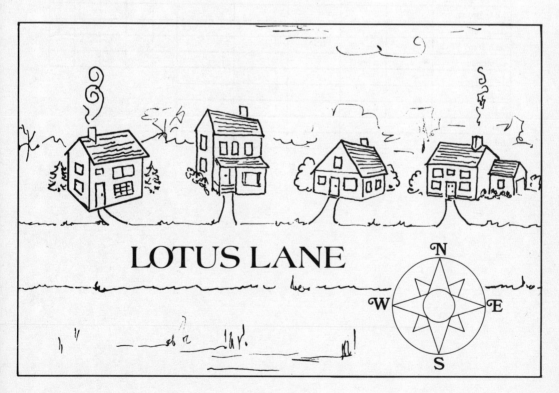

LOTUS LANE

N

W   E

S

6 RURAL MISHAPS

by Margaret Shoop

A butt by the family cow was one of the five different mishaps that befell Farmer Brown, his wife, his daughter, his teenage son, and his farmhand one summer morning. From the rhyme that follows, can you determine the mishap that happened to each of the five, and the order in which the events occurred?

1   The garter snake was surprised in a patch
2   And bit a grown man's finger.
3   One person who weeded a flower bed
4   Received a nasty stinger.
5   The farmer's mishap happened first;
6   Son Johnny's happened third.
7   When Mr. Reston was kicked by the mule,
8   He said, "My word! My word!"
9   The sting of the bee was the fourth mishap
10 To befall our rural cast.
11 Neither it nor the wasp attacked Mrs. Brown
12 Whose mishap wasn't the last.

The solution is on page 140.

	beesting	cow butt	mule kick	snake bite	wasp sting	1st	2nd	3rd	4th	5th
Farmer Brown										
Mrs. Brown										
daughter										
teen son										
farmhand										
1st										
2nd										
3rd										
4th										
5th										

7 THE GOLF COORDINATORS

by W. H. Organ

The Sunny Hills Country Club holds several intraclub golf matches each month. To assist the club's tournament director in conducting the matches, it is the custom for each golfing member to volunteer for a month's assignment as a tournament coordinator; a man is in charge of the men's events, a woman of the women's events, and when mixed events are scheduled, the two coordinators for the month cochair them. The list of the eight coordinators for September through December has just been posted; among them are Flag and John Ashe. From the following clues, can you determine the full names of each month's coordinators?

1. No mixed events are scheduled for December.

2. Bill Ambrose, whose assignment is not October, is scheduled for coordinator duties a month earlier than his wife Betty.

3. Maureen and Clark will be in charge of one mixed event, Betty and White another.

4. Shirley is not Wallace.

5. Dick's assignment is later than Bob's.

6. Ms. Morrison's assignment, which isn't December, is later than Dora's.

The solution is on page 140.

Remember: In this puzzle there are two coordinators for each month's matches, so when you find one coordinator for a month you cannot automatically put an X (no) in the rest of the boxes for that month until you ascertain the other coordinator.

	Ambrose	Ambrose	Ashe	Clark	Flag	Morrison	Wallace	White	Sept.	Oct.	Nov.	Dec.
Betty												
Bill												
Bob												
Dick												
Dora												
John												
Maureen												
Shirley												
Sept.												
Oct.												
Nov.												
Dec.												

8 READ THE FINE PRINT!

by Evelyn B. Rosenthal

Will and four other depositors at a bank found to their dismay that by not reading the fine print in the literature describing their accounts, they had let their balances fall too low and thereby incurred monthly charges, which were all whole numbers of dollars. From the following clues, can you find each one's full name (one surname is Carpenter), type of account (one is statement savings), and monthly charge?

1. Rhoda's last name is not Butler.

2. Edward was charged $1 less than the one with a super NOW account and $2 more than the one with a regular checking account.

3. Ms. Cook is not the one with a passbook savings account.

4. Taylor does not have a super NOW account.

5. Herbert was charged $8, Mason $4; of the other three, Gloria was charged less than the one with a NOW account and more than Butler.

6. The one with the NOW account was not charged the most, and Butler was not charged the least.

The solution is on page 141.

The boxes in the charges row and column have been left empty for you to fill in when you determine what they are.

	Butler	Carpenter	Cook	Mason	Taylor	NOW	passbook savings	reg. check.	state. savings	super NOW	charges		
Edward													
Gloria													
Herbert													
Rhoda													
Will													
charges													
NOW					
passbook savings					
reg. check.					
state. savings					
super NOW					

34

9 THE AQUARIUM VISIT

by Ellen K. Rodehorst

One day recently, Mrs. Green took her two children and her brother's two children to the Water World Aquarium. After seeing the show, the four children, including Daniel, told Mrs. Green which animal act they enjoyed the most. Each preferred a different act; one liked the walruses best. From the information below, can you discover each child's full name, age, and favorite animal act?

1. Matthew, who is not the child who liked the whales best, is the same age as one of his cousins.

2. One of the Brown brothers, who is not the child who liked the seals best, is five years old.

3. One child, who is six years old, did not like the whales.

4. The oldest child, who is seven years old, is not Tommy.

5. Sarah, who is not Tommy's cousin, is one year younger than the child who liked the dolphins best.

6. The child who liked the dolphins best is not Tommy.

The solution is on page 141.

We did not find a chart to be helpful in solving this puzzle. We suggest you use the space below to write down the facts as you establish them.

10 PICKLES, PEARS, AND PEACHES, PLUS

by Susan Zivich

Four sisters spent one afternoon canning food for the winter. Each sister canned four different foods, and no type of food was canned by more than two of the women. From the following information, can you determine what each sister canned?

1. Andrea canned pears.

2. Debbie canned beans but not peas.

3. Marcia made strawberry preserves, her favorite breakfast treat.

4. No one who canned corn also canned carrots.

5. Eleanor was not one of the sisters who canned pickles.

6. Only one of the sisters who canned corn also canned peas; Andrea canned neither.

7. Marcia and Eleanor both canned peaches.

8. No one canned both pickles and strawberry preserves.

9. Marcia did not can carrots.

The solution is on page 141.

The chart given below is probably the easiest way of keeping track of the information given in the clues. Remember, each sister canned four different foods.

	beans	carrots	corn	peaches	pears	peas	pickles	strawb.
Andrea								
Debbie								
Eleanor								
Marcia								

11 A PUZZLE PUZZLER

by Margaret Shoop

1	A book with three Logic Problems:
2	Number I, Number II, Number III,
3	Has each of the Ameses deducing
4	Though none has a logic degree.
5	The Ameses in number are seven,
6	Including each daughter and son.
7	No two solved just the same problems,
8	But each deduced at least one.
9	Your task: determine which problems
10	Each did with effort of will.
11	This rhyme has all the clues you need;
12	Just use your reasoning skill.
13	Problem III was not done by Cal,
14	By sweet Betsy, or by Dad;
15	And those who skipped Problem I
16	Included the teenager Brad.
17	Betsy and Cal each solved a problem
18	The other did not do,
19	And the same thing happened with Brad
20	And his lovely sister, smart Sue.
21	Sue gave some help to her small brother Cal
22	Who solved the problem marked I,
23	And Jimmy did just one of the three,
24	But found it a great deal of fun.
25	We have not mentioned Mrs. Ames,
26	But please do not omit 'er,
27	For you will find most certainly
28	That she was not a quitter.

The solution is on page 142.

The fill-in chart below is useful in keeping track of the information given in the clues.

		Mom	Dad	Betsy	Brad	Cal	Jimmy	Sue
puzzles solved	I							
	II							
	III							

12 002'S RENDEZVOUS

by Diane C. Baldwin

Agent 002 was gathering information from Carmen and three other ladies and arranged to meet each one separately at the fountain in the park, one at the stroke of each hour from 9:00 P.M. to midnight. So that he could recognize them quickly, he asked each to wear a different color dress (one was yellow). Since there were four paths leading to the fountain, from the north, south, east, and west, he had each lady use only one path, each different from that used by any of the others. From the following clues, can you tell when he met with each lady, what color each wore, and what path each took?

1. As Maria tiptoed toward the fountain, she could faintly see to her right the path a mysterious lady in green would take just an hour later.

2. The last lady on the scene was not dressed in red, nor did she steal into the park from east or west.

3. Tess and the lady in blue each arrived furtively an hour apart from opposite directions, as did two others who came an hour apart.

4. 002 saw his lady in blue, who did not take the west path, approach silently from the path which was to Enid's left, when she arrived an hour later.

The solution is on page 142.

We found this diagram of the park and its paths to be more helpful than the usual chart in solving this puzzle.

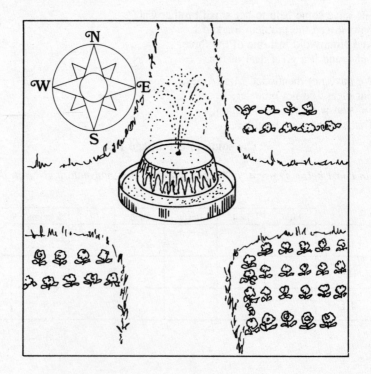

13 UNITED STATES STAMPS

by Evelyn B. Rosenthal

Many U.S. stamps have honored well-known people other than Presidents. Artists have even had their works depicted on stamps. From the following clues, can you determine the denominations of the stamps mentioned here and the people honored on them? *(Note: The stamps depicted here may or may not reflect those currently in use in the U.S. Postal Service. They are presented solely for the purpose of solving.)*

1. The Grandma Moses stamp cost 2¢ less than the Willa Cather stamp and 7¢ less than the Carl Sandburg stamp.

2. The John Sloan stamp cost 2¢ more than the Walt Disney stamp and 7¢ less than the Frances Perkins stamp.

3. The John Steinbeck stamp cost 2¢ more than the Harriet Tubman stamp and 7¢ more than the Willa Cather stamp.

4. The Dolley Madison stamp cost 7¢ more than the John Sloan stamp.

5. Three of the stamps cost 15¢ each and there are at least two of each other denomination.

The solution is on page 142.

Use this space for solving.

MEDIUM LOGIC PROBLEMS

14 THE AUBREY SISTERS

by Susan Zivich

Amy and the other four quintuplets, who are now in high school, have always been encouraged by their parents to pursue their own interests, with the result that the girls all play different musical instruments (one plays the harp), study different languages (one is learning Spanish), and collect different things (one collects stamps). From the following clues, can you determine each sister's interests?

1. The sister who is learning Russian collects old buttons.

2. The girl who plays the flute is studying German.

3. Anne collects coins.

4. Andrea, who plays the violin, is not learning French.

5. Last Saturday, Angela and the sister who collects rocks went shopping together, the one who plays the piano stayed home to practice, the one who studies French tutored a fellow student, and the one who plays the guitar rehearsed with an instrumental group.

6. The sister who collects butterflies plays the piano.

7. Alice is studying Italian.

The solution is on page 143.

name					
instrument					
language					
collection					

15 VIDEO ARCADE CONTEST

by Cheryl L. McLaughlin

Ten children, including Jessica, participated in a video arcade contest in which the children were paired off at five different games. From the clues below, can you determine each child's full name (one surname is Day) and the winner and loser at each video game?

1. Scott and the Booth boy were winners, along with the girl who played Starflight against Oscar, the Cole child, and Kate; neither the Cole child nor Kate played Submarines.

2. Doug, who didn't play Grabbin' Gators, won against the Hale boy, and Ginger defeated the Jarvis girl.

3. The Ellis boy, who isn't Nathan, lost to the Grant child.

4. The Aster child, who didn't play against the Keats child, was a winner, as was the Field boy.

5. Keith played Air Attack, Amy played Journey, and Cathy lost at Submarines.

The solution is on page 143.

The solution is on page 143.

WINNER			LOSER	
first name	last name	game	first name	last name
_____	_____	_____	_____	_____
_____	_____	_____	_____	_____
_____	_____	_____	_____	_____
_____	_____	_____	_____	_____
_____	_____	_____	_____	_____

44

16 THE WEBSTER CONNECTION

by W. H. Organ

To stimulate interest in the dictionary, Ms. Webster gave her English class a special homework assignment—to find two words in the dictionary they had never seen or heard of before. When the class assembled the next day, she selected Bella Long and five other children, including Bob and Cora, to define for the class the words they had found. From the following clues, can you determine their full names (one surname is Kern), the two new words each defined, and the order in which the six presented their definitions?

1. Amy, one of whose words was *nekton,* and the pupil who had chosen *clinquant* were the first two to give their definitions; Charles Palmer was next, followed by Don.

2. One of the girls defined *doppelgänger* and *locofoco*.

3. The Mason youngster, who was last, defined *pecksniffian*.

4. The Roper child defined the words *jugulum* and *thermotaxis*.

5. The Nagle boy was the first youngster to give his definitions; one of his words was *sapsago*.

6. One of the pupils defined *hippogriff* and *whiffet*.

7. *Acrophobia* was defined before *gallipot*.

The solution is on page 143.

	1st	2nd	3rd	4th	5th	6th
first name						
last name						
words						

17 HELPING THE ELDERLY

by Diane Yoko

The Young boy and four other teenagers in Sunrise Valley volunteer their Saturdays to help the elderly. None will accept a cash payment for his service, but the recipients usually insist on giving the helpers a homemade gift; last Saturday, one got chocolate chip cookies. From the following clues, try to determine each boy's full name and age, the job he did last Saturday (one boy painted a fence, and another mowed a lawn), and the gift he received.

1. Three of the boys—a fourteen-year-old (whose gift was fudge), Bobby, and the Smith boy—did painting.

2. Neither the Bailey boy nor the Illes boy, who isn't the one who painted a garage, was the one who got the apple pie.

3. Pete, whose last name isn't Bailey, is one year younger than the boy who grocery-shopped, who is one year younger than Carl, who didn't paint.

4. The boy whose gift was oatmeal cookies didn't paint the garage.

5. Pete and the Smith boy are the same age.

6. Kenny's gift was neither the oatmeal cookies nor the scarf.

7. Andy is not the boy who painted shutters, and his gift was not a scarf.

8. Andy is two years younger than the boy whose gift was an apple pie.

9. The Norton boy and the boy who grocery-shopped are the same age.

The solution is on page 144.

Because of the size of this chart, it had to be divided in two, but it is used in the normal way for solving.

	Bailey	Illes	Norton	Smith	Young	groc. shop	paint fence	paint gar.	paint shut.	mow lawn	apple pie	ch.ch. cookies	fudge	oat. cook.	scarf
Andy															
Bobby															
Carl															
Kenny															
Pete															
ages															
apple pie															
ch.ch. cookies															
fudge															
oat. cook.															
scarf															
groc. shop															
paint fence															
paint gar.															
paint shut.															
mow lawn															

	ages				
Andy					
Bobby					
Carl					
Kenny					
Pete					

18 REAL ESTATE

by Ellen K. Rodehorst

A large real estate office did brisk business last week. Five of the agents, including Robert, closed sales on five different-style homes. Five couples, including the Meyers, bought homes, one of which was a ranch style, from five different sellers (including the Reids). No two of the final selling prices, one of which was $92,000, were the same. From the details given below, can you coordinate the real estate agent, buyer, seller, style of home, and selling price involved in each transaction?

1. Jane, who didn't deal with the Taylors, did not sell the $63,000 home.

2. The Bakers did not sell their home to the Halls.

3. The Adamses paid twice as much for their new home as the amount Debbie finally got for the Flynns' home, which was not the trilevel.

4. The condominium, which was not the home the Simons bought, was not the home that sold for $46,000.

5. One couple, who were not the Meyers, paid an amount for their new home that was as much less than the price the Spears sold their home for as it was more than what the Halls finally paid.

6. Alice had no dealings with the Uptons.

7. The Taylors couldn't afford the $80,000 asking price for the duplex, but the agent, who wasn't Alice, convinced the seller to take $4000 less to close the sale.

8. Jack, who wasn't working for the Uptons, managed to get $50,000 for the beach cottage.

The solution is on page 144.

agent	seller	style	buyer	price
_____	_____	_____	_____	_____
_____	_____	_____	_____	_____
_____	_____	_____	_____	_____
_____	_____	_____	_____	_____
_____	_____	_____	_____	_____

19 HOLIDAZE

by Vivian Gail Collins

The records at Hope Memorial Hospital show that several sets of twins were born there in the preceding year. Of those, six sets, including the Barnes twins, were born on holidays, although no two sets were born on the same day. Each of these six sets had a different combined birth weight; these weights ranged from seven to ten pounds. From the clues below, can you figure out the full names of all six pairs of twins (two first names are Kevin and Mary), when each pair was born, and how much each pair weighed?

1. Carol and her twin Jason, who were not born February 14th, had the lowest combined birth weight.

2. No girls were born on March 17th and no boys on July 4th.

3. The combined weight of the Hollis twins was nine and a half pounds.

4. Becky and her brother together weighed seven and a half pounds and were born on December 25th.

5. John Allen and his sister, who is not Susan or Patty, together weighed one pound more than the twins born January 1st.

6. The twins born October 31st together weighed eight pounds.

7. David and his twin together weighed one pound more than the Stuart girls.

8. Kathy and her sister, who isn't Susan, are older than Brad Wilkes but younger than Debra Taylor.

The solution is on page 145.

	first names		last name	weight
Jan. 1				
Feb. 14				
Mar. 17				
July 4				
Oct. 31				
Dec. 25				

20 AT THE COUNTY FAIR

by Haydon Calhoun

One Saturday, Joe and four of his friends attended the Cool County Fair. Each had a different amount of money to spend—at least $10, but no more than $20. From the clues below, can you determine the amount of money each boy had and the amount he spent? *(Note: All amounts are in whole dollars; there are no cents figures involved.)*

1. The boy who spent $11 spent $2 more than he had left.

2. Dan spent twice as much as he had left.

3. Bud, Ken, and Tim each spent the same amount as each of them had left.

4. One boy started with an odd number of dollars.

5. Dan had the same amount left as Tim.

6. Bud spent $1 more than Tim.

7. Ken started with $8 more than one other boy had left.

The solution is on page 145.

Use this space for solving.

21 BRIDAL ATTENDANTS

by Carolyne McKinney

Reverend Jones married five couples during the month of June. He noted that each bride had a different number of attendants (each had at least one). From the following clues you should be able to determine the first and last name of each couple as well as the number of attendants each bride had.

1. Carla had two more attendants than Gary's bride, who had two more than Mrs. Morris.

2. Doris's and Mrs. Oliver's attendants added together equaled the number Isaac's bride had; Mrs. Oliver did not have the fewest.

3. Jack's bride had more attendants than Frank's; the latter is not Anna.

4. Mrs. Kelly had twice as many attendants as Howard's bride; together, they had as many as Ellen, who had half as many as Mrs. Neuman.

5. Neither Betty nor Doris was the bride with only one attendant.

6. Mrs. Likens had more attendants than at least one of the other brides.

The solution is on page 146.

number of attendants	bride's name	groom's name	last name
_____	_____	_____	_____
_____	_____	_____	_____
_____	_____	_____	_____
_____	_____	_____	_____

22 ONCE AROUND WILDE LAKE

by Diane C. Baldwin

Sachs and three other people who were in Wilde Lake Park at the same time each circled the lake once while pursuing a different pastime (one was bird-watching) and eventually passed the main dock. From the following clues, can you give each person's full name and pastime, as well as the order in which the four reached the dock?

1. The person pushing the baby carriage, who wasn't Margot, proceeded around the lake counterclockwise, as did Pratt; neither overtook the other.

2. Jerry, who isn't Bosen, overtook the dog walker just after she passed the dock and just before she came face-to-face with someone coming from the other direction, who wasn't Jill.

3. As she caught her first view of the dock, Jill could see the jogger passing Margot and coming toward her.

4. Meg and the jogger, neither of whom is Chang, proceeded clockwise around the lake.

The solution is on page 146.

We found the diagram of the lake opposite to be the most helpful in solving this puzzle.

	first name	last name	pastime
First			
Second			
Third			
Fourth			

23 FLOWERS FOR THE DANCE

by Evelyn B. Rosenthal

John and two other boys each bought his date a corsage for a school prom and a boutonniere to match the corsage for himself. Thus, the boy who gave his date a corsage of red roses wore a red flower in his lapel. Each danced the first dance with his date—one was Donna—and then exchanged partners for the second and third dances, so that each had danced with all three girls by the end of the third dance. From the following clues, can you find each girl's full name (the last name of one is Cox), her corsage, her escort's full name (one surname is Sloan), and her partners for the second and third dances?

1. The girl wearing the purple orchid corsage was Rob's partner for the second dance and the Evans boy's for the third.

2. Bea danced the second dance with the Rowe boy and the third with the boy wearing the white boutonniere.

3. The Harris girl's second partner was the boy with the red boutonniere, and her third George.

4. Neither Ann nor the Marsh girl wore the white gardenia corsage.

The solution is on page 146.

girl	flower color	1st dance	2nd dance	3rd dance

24 THE RHYMESTERS

by W. H. Organ

Ms. Tennyson's class was having its first lesson in rhyming. As an exercise, she gave the youngsters the first lines of two different couplets and asked them to make up second lines which would rhyme with the first. One given line ended with the word *fame,* the other with the word *roam.* She told her pupils that the first six to finish could read their compositions to the class. From the following clues, can you determine the full names of the six children (one first name is Roger), the order in which they finished, and the two rhyming words (one was *name* and one was *dome*) chosen by each?

1. The three who finished first were Joe, whose last name is not Kilmer; then the pupil who used the word *tame;* and then the girl who used the word *home.*

2. Bess Longfellow, who used *gnome* as one of her words, was last of the six to finish.

3. Ellen used *game* in one of her lines and *loam* in the other.

4. The Kilmer child, who used *comb,* finished before Dick, who used *aim* and whose last name is not Keats.

5. The Shelley child, who used *dame,* is not the one who used *foam* or the one who used *home.*

6. Amy is not the one who used *blame.*

7. The Whittier child finished before the Keats child, who finished before the Burns child.

The solution is on page 147.

	first name	last name		words
1.	_____	_____	_____	_____
2.	_____	_____	_____	_____
3.	_____	_____	_____	_____
4.	_____	_____	_____	_____
5.	_____	_____	_____	_____
6.	_____	_____	_____	_____

25 MRS. FINNEGAN'S BOARDERS

by W. H. Organ

Preparing breakfast for Will and her five other boarders before they set out for work each morning keeps Mrs. Finnegan very busy. Her task is made somewhat easier, however, by the fact that each young man has the same breakfast every morning—either eggs or pancakes, accompanied by either bacon, ham, or sausage. Each one also has either coffee, tea, or milk. No two have exactly the same breakfast. It should be added that Mrs. Finnegan has a firm rule: She will not prepare any dish for only one person. From the following clues, can you determine what each boarder has for breakfast?

1. Al, who does not like sausage, usually sits next to the boarder who breakfasts on bacon and pancakes.

2. Bob and Chuck both have ham.

3. Peter does not care for bacon.

4. Ned does not like pancakes.

5. Bob has coffee.

6. The sausage eaters have tea; two of the pancake eaters have coffee; the other two boarders drink milk.

7. More than two of the boarders have eggs.

The solution is on page 147.

The solution is on page 147.

	eggs	pancakes	bacon	ham	sausage	coffee	tea	milk
Al								
Bob								
Chuck								
Ned								
Peter								
Will								

26 IT'S A TRIP

by Cheryl L. McLaughlin

The Wileys and four other couples vacationed aboard five different State Sea cruise liners; one ship was the *New York*. Each couple visited two ports, but no two couples visited the same two ports. From the following clues, can you determine the full names of each couple (one man is Mike and one woman is Goldie), the name of their ship, and the two ports each visited?

1. John and his wife Bev visited Hawaii, as the Becks did also, and the Bahamas, as did Wilma Eastman and her husband.

2. June and her husband, who isn't Dave, went to St. Thomas, as did the couple who traveled aboard the *California*.

3. Jim and his wife traveled aboard the *Illinois* and went to Tahiti, as did the Eastmans, and also to Bermuda, as did Burt and his wife Mary, who are neither the Becks nor the Simpsons.

4. The Taylors traveled aboard the *Montana;* the *Washington* made a stop in Hawaii.

The solution is on page 147.

wife	husband	last name	ship	ports of call
_____	_____	_____	_____	_____ & _____
_____	_____	_____	_____	_____ & _____
_____	_____	_____	_____	_____ & _____
_____	_____	_____	_____	_____ & _____
_____	_____	_____	_____	_____ & _____

27 REDECORATING

by Diane Yoko

Ms. Riley and four other women are homeowners on the same block of Cypress Street. Their addresses are 103, 105, and 107 on the north side of the street, and 104 and 106 on the south side. Each woman is redecorating a different room in her home (one is a living room), and each has made a different major purchase (one bought paneling). From the following clues, try to determine the full name of the woman at each address, what each purchased, and what room she is redecorating.

1. Three women—Flo, the one who is redecorating her bathroom, and the one who bought bamboo shades—live on the same side of the street; the other two, Ms. Mitchell and the woman who purchased a chandelier, live on the other side.

2. Kit's house number is higher than Ms. Tuley's, whose number is higher than that of the woman who is redecorating her study, who isn't Flo.

3. The chandelier isn't for the bedroom.

4. Dee and the woman who purchased the mirror tiles live on the same side of the street but are not immediate neighbors.

5. Ms. Swift, who isn't Jan, has a higher house number than the one who is redecorating her kitchen but a lower one than Ms. Lynch; Ms. Tuley is not redecorating her kitchen.

6. Bev is a next-door neighbor of the woman who bought the carpeting, whose address is the highest.

The solution is on page 148.

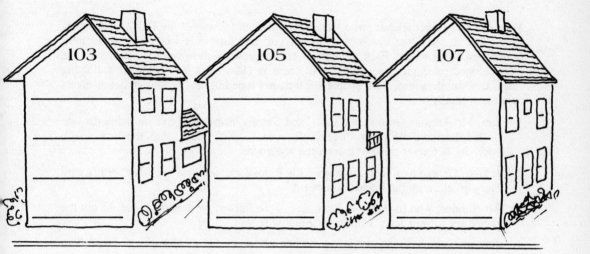

CYPRESS STREET

28 GENTLEMEN CHEFS

by W. H. Organ

Myra and five of her friends, who live along the ninth fairway of the Oak Tree Country Club, have at least two things in common: golf and husbands who boast about their prowess in the kitchen. Each gentleman chef's prowess, however, is limited to the preparation of a single specialty; one of these is clam chowder. From the following clues, can you determine each couple's full names (one husband is Joe) and each man's culinary specialty?

1. Jim, Mr. Parsons (who is not Max), and Carol's husband all live on the north side of the fairway; the other three chefs— Jack, Mr. Baker, and the one whose specialty is Caesar salad— live on the south side.

2. It takes George two hours to prepare his Brunswick stew and one hour for his wife Doris to clean up the kitchen afterward.

3. Mr. Linden, who lives on the south side of the fairway, makes nut bread; he got the recipe for it from Jane, who is not Jim's wife.

4. Jane and her husband, who is not the one whose specialty is sourdough bread, live next door to the Joneses.

5. Matt Jones's specialty is meat loaf.

6. Mr. Clark and George live on opposite sides of the fairway.

7. Betty, who is not Mrs. Roper, and Penny live on the same side of the fairway.

The solution is on page 148.

	George	Jack	Jim	Joe	Matt	Max	last names B	C	J	L	P	R	chow.	meat loaf	nut bread	s.d. bread	salad	stew
Betty																		
Carol																			
Doris																			
Jane																			
Myra																			
Penny																			
chow.																			
meat loaf																			
nut bread																			
s.d. bread																			
salad																			
stew																			

last names		George	Jack	Jim	Joe	Matt	Max
	B						
	C						
	J						
	L						
	P						
	R						

29 TRACTS AND TREES

by W. H. Organ

The new tract which a development company has recently opened up in Oakmont has proved most attractive to potential buyers; seven, including Barnes, have already made substantial down payments on lots. In the sales agreements, the developer has promised to plant two trees on each of the lots, the types of trees to be chosen by the new owner. From the following clues, can you determine each buyer's down payment and choice of trees?

1. Each of the buyers chose a fruit tree as one of his trees.

2. The down payments were all multiples of $500; none exceeded $4,000, none was less than $1,500, and only two were in the same amount.

3. Brady chose a cypress as one of his trees; his down payment was $2,000 more than that of Newton, who chose a lemon tree and a cypress.

4. Hammer, who chose a plum tree, made a down payment which was half that made by the buyer who chose a lemon and an elm.

5. Parks, who was the only one to make a down payment of $2,000, chose an elm as one of his trees; the other was not a cherry.

6. Allerton's down payment was larger than that of the buyer who chose a lemon tree and a pine but not as large as that of Sloan, who chose an elm.

7. Two of the buyers chose cherry trees; among the other trees selected were at least one lime and at least one oak.

The solution is on page 148.

The solution is on page 148.

buyer	down payment	trees	
_____	$_____	_____ &	_____
_____	$_____	_____ &	_____
_____	$_____	_____ &	_____
_____	$_____	_____ &	_____
_____	$_____	_____ &	_____
_____	$_____	_____ &	_____
_____	$_____	_____ &	_____

30 REQUEST TIME

by Julie Spence

Barry and the other four male members of the Rock Old Style Band are always happy to take requests to play "oldies but goodies." Before the band began playing at their last gig, Barb and four other women each talked to a different member of the band and made a request for a special song. No two of the women requested the same song; one asked for "Wake Up My Pillow." From the information below, can you determine what song each woman requested of which band member, what instrument each band member plays (one plays saxophone), and in what order the songs were requested? *(Note: The lead singer is the only band member who does not play an instrument; each of the others plays only one instrument.)*

1. Jane made her request after the woman who requested "Smoke Gets in the Wind" and just before the woman who asked Eric for a song.

2. Nola made her request before the woman who asked Chris for a song.

3. One woman requested "Tears on the Clock" just after Trudy made her request and before anyone had talked to Mark.

4. The piano player took a request after Sue made her request.

5. Andy and the guitar player were both taking their instruments out of their cases when they overheard a woman asking the drummer to play "Rock Around Little Susie." These two received requests later.

6. "Blowin' in Your Eyes" was requested before at least two other songs.

The solution is on page 149.

	song	requested by	band member	instrument
1				
2				
3				
4				
5				

31   BEINGS FROM ANOTHER GALAXY

by Diane Yoko

In a galaxy many, many light years away, Ando and four other yonixes (astronauts to us) from different planets stopped at the intergalactic fuel station to replenish their spaceships' supplies of fuel pellets. Each yonix has a different-color spaceship; one is silver. From the following clues, can you deduce each yonix's planet and spaceship-color and tell how many fuel pellets each bought?

1. The yonix from the planet Zucon bought ten fewer fuel pellets than the one whose spaceship is orange.

2. The yonix from the planet Pluriz, who isn't Boiz, bought more than twice as many fuel pellets as Uris, whose spaceship isn't the green one.

3. The yonix who bought fifty fuel pellets has a purple spaceship.

4. Exis, whose spaceship isn't purple, isn't the yonix from the planet Quazin.

5. The yonix in the blue spaceship is from the planet Tyrus.

6. The yonix from the planet Diatis bought twenty fuel pellets, half as many as the one whose spaceship is orange and twice as many as Droc.

The solution is on page 149.

	Diatis	Pluriz	Quazin	Tyrus	Zucon	blue	green	orange	purple	silver	number of pellets					
Ando																
Boiz																
Droc																
Exis																
Uris																
number of pellets																
blue																
green																
orange																
purple																
silver																

32 ADDISON FAIR FOOD COMPETITION

by Diane C. Baldwin

Ms. Sims and four other women wait anxiously outside the food tent at the Addison County Fair. Inside, their five entries (one is preserves) are lined up in a row for tasting and final judging. The judges are placing a different ribbon by each one signifying grand prize, first prize, second prize, third prize, or honorable mention. Who will get the best—Myra, Irene, or one of the others? The tent flap is opening now. From the following clues, can you find the full name of the winner of each prize, her entry, and the position of her entry on the judging table?

1. Marion's entry is not next to that of a woman whose first name begins with the same letter as hers.

2. To the left of June, there are two entries before you reach the pie. Ms. Block's (which has not won second prize) is directly to the left of June's entry and none of these has won the grand prize.

3. May's entry, which is not the pickles, is between Ms. Ives's entry and the layer cake.

4. The entry that has received first prize is between Marion's and Ms. Martin's entries; none of these is the tarts.

5. Ms. Wilson's entry has three entries between it and the one which won honorable mention, but only one between hers and the one which won second prize; neither Ms. Wilson's entry nor the honorable mention nor the second-prize winner is the layer cake.

The solution is on page 150.

WINNERS' TABLE

Entered by

_____

_____

Entry

Entered by

_____

_____

Entry

Entered by

_____

_____

Entry

Entered by

_____

_____

Entry

Entered by

_____

_____

Entry

33 THE PRINCESSES AND THE DRAGONS

by Susan Zivich

The Princess of Shropshire and three other princesses were captured by four ferocious dragons. Luckily, they were rescued by four brave princes, including Prince Nathan; one of the four was the Prince of Chippenham. From the following clues, can you match each princess (and her kingdom) with the fire-breathing dragon who captured her and the prince (and his kingdom) who rescued her?

1. Princess Genevieve, who was rescued by the Prince of Nottingham, was not the one captured by the dragon called Brujo.

2. The Prince of Durham fought the dragon called Shrayik.

3. Prince Geoffrey rescued the Princess of Cheshire.

4. Princess Catherine was held captive by the dragon called Trollkarl.

5. Winifred was the Princess of Lancashire.

6. Prince Lionel rescued Princess Regina.

7. Prince Erwin lived in Huntingham.

8. The dragon called Gespent captured the Princess of Berkshire.

The solution is on page 150.

Because of the size of the solving chart, it had to be divided in two. It is used in the normal way, however.

	Berkshire	Cheshire	Lancashire	Shropshire	Brujo	Gespent	Shrayik	Trollkarl	Erwin	Geoffrey	Lionel	Nathan
Catherine												
Genevieve												
Regina												
Winifred												
Chippenham												
Durham												
Huntingham												
Nottingham												
Erwin												
Geoffrey												
Lionel												
Nathan												
Brujo												
Gespent												
Shrayik												
Trollkarl												

	Chippenham	Durham	Huntingham	Nottingham
Catherine				
Genevieve				
Regina				
Winifred				

67

34 VACATION VISITS

by Diane C. Baldwin

Mother and Dad visited their four daughters (one of whom is Alice) and sons-in-law (one of whom is Dave) while they vacationed; one of the couples lives in Columbia. From the information below, can you determine the order of the visits, each couple's full names (one surname is Gold), and the town where each lives?

1. The visit to Annie and her husband came just before the one to Bill and his wife; neither couple lives in Madison.

2. The first visit wasn't to Sally and her husband, who aren't the couple from Concord, or to Jane and her husband.

3. The last visit wasn't to see Bruce and his wife.

4. The Chatham visit preceded the one to Mrs. Baker, who isn't Sally.

5. Mr. Smith, who wasn't the last son-in-law visited, isn't Bob.

6. The visit to the Wangs came before the one to Madison, which was directly followed by the visit to Bruce and his wife.

7. The visit to the Bakers came later than the one to Jane and her husband.

The solution is on page 150.

	Bill	Bob	Bruce	Dave	Baker	Gold	Smith	Wang
Alice								
Annie								
Jane								
Sally								

	daughter	"son"	last name	city
1st visit				
2nd visit				
3rd visit				
4th visit				

35 RECOGNITION DINNER

by Julie Spence

Last week, the Gibbon Company held a recognition dinner for Brian, Carol, and three other employees who were leaving their positions for various reasons. From the clues below, can you determine the full name of each honoree (one surname is Norris), the number of years each had been with the company (all were different whole numbers of years), and the reason each was leaving his or her current position?

1. The one who had been with Gibbon the fewest number of years, 10, received a position with a different company.

2. Frank had been with Gibbon 5 years longer than Crosby, who had been with the company twice as long as Mr. Miller.

3. Shirley and Anderson both received promotions within the company.

4. Wolfe had been with the company twice as long as Doreen, who had been with Gibbon 5 years longer than one of the others.

5. The two who had been with Gibbon the longest, neither over 50 years, were both retiring.

The solution is on page 151.

Use this space for solving.

36 SWEETS AND STUDIES

by Susan Zivich

Rita and five of her classmates were seated around a round table, studying and each munching a different kind of cookie; one was eating chocolate chip cookies. Although everyone had more than one cookie, no one had more than eight, and no two ate the same number. From the following clues, can you figure out the seating arrangement and how many of what kind of cookie each girl ate?

1. The student who ate the peanut-butter cookies ate twice as many cookies as the girl to her left.

2. Jill sat between the student who ate marshmallow cookies and the student who ate three cookies.

3. Pam ate three times as many cookies as the student directly across from her.

4. Mary sat next to the student who ate the butterscotch cookies and directly across from the student who ate the peanut-butter cookies.

5. Dolly ate more cookies than Sharon, but fewer than Pam; Dolly is not the one who ate the lemon bars.

6. Sharon ate twice as many cookies as the student on her right but only half as many as the student who ate the oatmeal cookies.

The solution is on page 151.

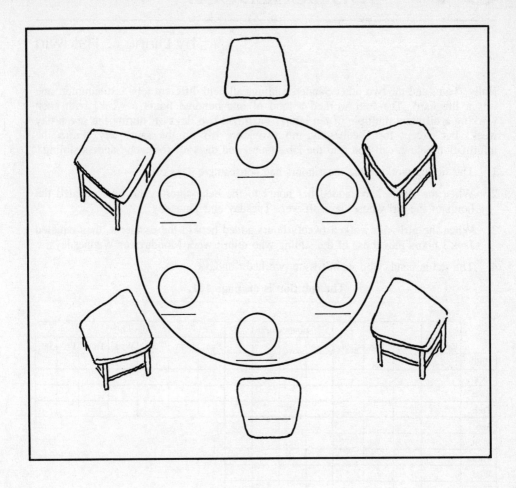

37 SUMMER JOB SCHEDULE

by Diane C. Baldwin

Holly, Tom, and the two other Sanders siblings all held different jobs last summer; one was a lifeguard. The four worked a total of one hundred hours a week, with each working a different multiple of ten hours. Each had two days off during the seven-day week, but except for Wednesday, no two were off on the same day. From the information below, can you find the job, hours, and days off for each Sanders sibling?

1. The sibling working the most hours had consecutive days off.

2. When the stable hand added her hours to the baby-sitter's, the total equaled the hours of the girl whose days off were Tuesday and Thursday.

3. When the girl who worked twenty hours added hers to the cashier's, they equaled Jack's hours plus those of the sibling who didn't work Mondays or Wednesdays.

4. The stable hand, who wasn't Kate, worked Sundays.

The solution is on page 151.

	baby-sit	cash.	lifeg.	stable	hours worked				Sun.	Mon.	Tues.	Wed.	Thur.	Fri.	Sat.
Holly															
Jack															
Kate															
Tom															
Sun.															
Mon.															
Tues.															
Wed.															
Thur.															
Fri.															
Sat.															
hrs. worked															

72

38 VICTORY AT SUNRISE VALLEY HIGH

by Diane Yoko

In the final play-off of the regional basketball tournament, the Sunrise Valley High Scorpions won with a record score of 75 points. One member of the team is the Hudson boy. From the clues that follow, try to determine each player's full name and position and the number of points he scored. *(Note: On a basketball team, there are two forwards, two guards, and one center.)*

1. The Nelson boy scored five points more than Luke but fewer than one of the guards.

2. Danny scored ten points more than the Benson boy, who scored twice as many as Rob.

3. Luke scored fifteen points.

4. Lenny doesn't play forward.

5. The center scored ten points fewer than Vince, who scored the greatest number of points.

6. The Stevens boy scored fewer points than the Carson boy, who is not a guard.

The solution is on page 152.

The solution is on page 152.

points	first name	last name	position
_____	_____	_____	_____
_____	_____	_____	_____
_____	_____	_____	_____
_____	_____	_____	_____
_____	_____	_____	_____

39 THE THREE-LEGGED RACE

by Randall L. Whipkey

At this year's Summerset Playground sports day, the children were divided into five teams for the competitions. Lisa was one of the youngsters in the three-legged race, in which one boy and one girl represented each team. From the clues below, can you identify each team's contestants and the order of finish in the event?

1. Jack and Karen were not partners.

2. Chad and his partner finished just ahead of Mandy and hers, who finished ahead of the yellow team.

3. The red team finished one place ahead of the blue team, of which David wasn't a member.

4. Jack wasn't on the orange team.

5. Gary and his teammate finished just ahead of Karen's team, which wasn't last.

6. Ian and Sara were partners, but they were not on the yellow team.

7. David and his partner finished just ahead of the green team's pair, who finished one place ahead of Jill and her teammate.

8. Gary wasn't on the red team.

The solution is on page 152.

	Jill	Karen	Lisa	Mandy	Sara	blue	green	orange	red	yellow	1	2	3	4	5
Chad															
David															
Gary															
Ian															
Jack															
1										
2										
3										
4										
5										
blue					
green					
orange					
red					
yellow					

	boy	girl	color
1st place	_____	_____	_____
2nd place	_____	_____	_____
3rd place	_____	_____	_____
4th place	_____	_____	_____
5th place	_____	_____	_____

HARD LOGIC PROBLEMS

40 SOMETHING TO DO

by Nancy R. Patterson

When rain kept all five Bouncy boys indoors one Saturday, they complained to their mother that they had nothing to do. In response, Mrs. Bouncy assigned each son a different chore: one boy was to brush the dog. Naturally, each child thought up something of his own to do when he had finished his chore, rather than ask Mother again! From the clues below, can you figure out what chore each boy did, and what activity he then devised for himself?

1. Jerry and Larry finished their chores before the other three: the youngest, the oldest, and the one who chose to make a poster.

2. Barry, who isn't the oldest, didn't empty wastebaskets.

3. The five boys are Harry, the two told to "Empty wastebaskets!" and "Oil your skates!," and the two who chose to work a jigsaw puzzle and build a model.

4. The youngest child, who isn't Gary, amused himself by looking at rooms upside down; he wasn't assigned oiling skates.

5. The oldest child was assigned to knock down cobwebs; he didn't do a jigsaw puzzle.

6. The boy who had to wipe off the light switches isn't Harry.

7. Jerry isn't the boy who amused himself by putting on his raincoat and practicing foul shots.

The solution is on page 152.

The solution is on page 152.

	remove cobwebs	brush dog	oil skates	wipe switches	empty baskets	foul shots	jigsaw	model	poster	upside down	oldest	youngest
Barry												
Gary												
Harry												
Jerry												
Larry												
oldest												
young.												
foul shots												
jigsaw												
model												
poster												
upside down												

41 WEEKEND EXCURSION

by W. R. Pinkston

Three married couples in Dallas, including Ted and his wife, were looking forward to a weekend together on an excursion to Las Vegas, when they received word that their direct flight had been canceled. The travel agent said seats were available for three of the six on a flight going and returning via Phoenix and added that three seats were also available on an equivalent flight with stopovers at El Paso. The group agreed to this alternative, and after much discussion as to how the group would divide, one of the women, Eva, suggested they draw slips from a hat for outbound flight assignments, with another drawing for the return flights. This line of action was followed; the Deans and the other two couples all had enjoyable weekends. From the following clues, can you find the couples' full names and determine how each person traveled to and from Las Vegas? *(Note: All three of the women have adopted their husbands' surnames.)*

1. On one return flight, two of the men and Ann were together.

2. One flight included Mr. and Mrs. Wells plus another of the men; the latter was not Bob.

3. Both of Bob's flights were via Phoenix.

4. One flight included Sam, Mrs. Smith, and Sue. Sam's wife was not on the plane.

5. Sue and her husband plus another woman were together on one return flight.

The solution is on page 153.

OUTGOING VIA _____

_____

_____

_____

RETURN VIA _____

_____

_____

_____

OUTGOING VIA _____

_____

_____

_____

RETURN VIA _____

_____

_____

_____

42   SEE HOW THEY SAT

by Susan Zivich

Four couples went to dinner together; they were seated at a round table and, although each man sat between two women, no man sat next to his wife. One of the eight is a senator. Can you figure out the full names and occupations of all eight diners and find their seating arrangement?

1. Mrs. Sawyer is a ski instructor, and Scott is a sculptor.

2. Mr. Stewart sat between Stephanie and the salesperson.

3. Steve is married to the songwriter.

4. Sally sat to the statistician's immediate left and directly opposite Mrs. Stewart.

5. Mrs. Shepherd's first name is Sarah.

6. Sam was seated between Mrs. Stanton and the sociologist.

7. Stan sat directly opposite the stockbroker.

8. Susan was seated to the right of Mr. Shepherd.

The solution is on page 153.

insert art pg 119

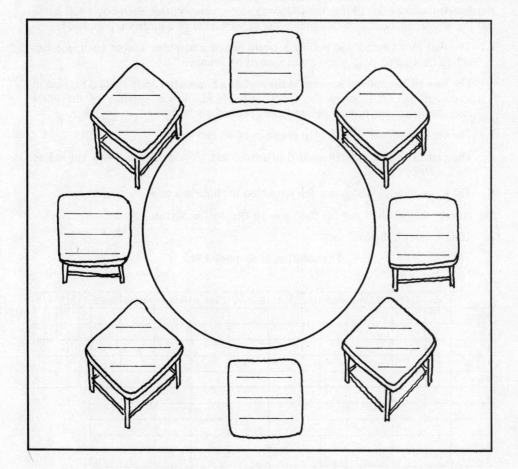

43 TINY BIRD WATCHERS

by Mary A. Powell

One morning, Jimmy and four other little boys decided to become bird watchers. Although they didn't know the names of very many birds, each did manage to identify one bird, with the identifications confirmed by Jimmy's mother; one of the boys spotted a redheaded woodpecker. From the following clues, can you find each boy's full name and the bird he spotted, as well as the order in which the five birds were spotted?

1. The first bird spotted was pulling a worm out of a neighbor's front lawn, the last sitting on a fence post; neither was spotted by Johnny.

2. The Howell boy spotted his bird on the roof of a house after Jerry spotted his bird in a walnut tree, but before the red-winged blackbird was spotted; of the other two, the robin was spotted before Lenny spotted his bird.

3. The crow was spotted in the top branches of an elm tree.

4. The pigeon, which was not spotted in a tree, was spotted after the crow but before the Smith boy's bird.

5. The Caswell boy, who is not Jerry, spotted his bird in a tree.

6. Neither the first bird nor the third was spotted by the Martin boy.

7. Tony is not the Boswell boy.

The solution is on page 154.

	crow	pigeon	blackbird	robin	woodpeck.	Boswell	Caswell	Howell	Martin	Smith	1	2	3	4	5
Jerry															
Jimmy															
Johnny															
Lenny															
Tony															
1															
2															
3															
4															
5															
Boswell															
Caswell															
Howell															
Martin															
Smith															

44 SCHOOL LUNCHES

by Evelyn B. Rosenthal

The McGee boy and three others who brought lunch to school traded among themselves so that each ended up with a different sandwich and a different dessert from those he brought. From the following clues, can you find the full name of each boy, the sandwich and dessert (one was a cupcake) he brought, and those he ended with?

1. The boy who brought the ham sandwich brought a piece of fruit for dessert; the boy who ate the ham sandwich ate a piece of fruit for dessert.

2. Lew and the Archer boy, who is not Tony, did not have a bologna sandwich either before or after the trades.

3. One boy had a peanut butter sandwich and an apple to start with, and another ended up with a cheese sandwich and a banana.

4. Walt and the Fry boy did not have a ham sandwich either before or after the trades.

5. One boy ended with a bologna sandwich and a doughnut.

6. Mike and the Lowe boy did not have a cheese sandwich either before or after the trades.

7. No lunch remained intact after the trades.

The solution is on page 154.

first name	last name	sandwich brought	dessert brought	sandwich eaten	dessert eaten

45 CENTER CIRCLE FAMILIES

by Cheryl L. McLaughlin

The Cannons and four other families who live on Center Circle have among them a total of fifteen children, including Jack, John, Luke, Gina, and Jill; each family has a different number of children. One father is Brad, and one child is Tim Baldwin. From the clues, can you determine the full names of all five families?

1. Robert, who isn't Mr. Scorps, has two daughters and three sons.

2. Rick and his wife Leslie, who aren't the Webers, have children with identical initials.

3. Lisa Scorps has three brothers; neither Ron Vernon nor Bob has any.

4. Gayle has more children than Jenny, who has more children than Holly, who isn't Mrs. Vernon.

5. Vickie, who isn't married to Lenny, has one child of each sex.

6. Barb and Laura are sisters, and Scott and Billy are brothers; Wayne and Ben's son Sam aren't related.

The solution is on page 155.

Use this space for solving.

46 WINTER PAGEANT

by Nancy R. Patterson

Children at the Exurbia Community School recently delighted their parents with a winter pageant. After the first-graders opened the program with "Jingle Bells," Joel, Judy, and three other youngsters from grades two through six presented a short play they had written, which included a character named Starlight. One child from each grade performed each of the five roles in the play, one of which was a fawn, one of the more difficult characters to costume. From the clues below, can you determine each child's grade, the character each played, and the character's name? *(Note: You may assume throughout that the higher the grade, the older the child.)*

1. The five children are the girl who played the fairy, the child who played Hollyberry, the fifth-grader, the one who played the squirrel, and Amy.

2. Although not the oldest, the child who played Candlewick is older than Martin.

3. The two youngest children had no lines.

4. The children who played Peppermint and the elf are both older than the one who played Snowflake the bunny, who is older than one of the girls.

5. Sally forgot one of her lines, failing to give the child who played Peppermint an entrance cue.

6. The fairy gave the closing speech: "Winter brings us fun and beauty."

The solution is on page 155.

	name	character	character's name
2nd grade			
3rd grade			
4th grade			
5th grade			
6th grade			

47 NURSERY SCHOOL PICNIC

by Mary A. Powell

Earl and the other nine children at Sunny Day Nursery School were taken on a picnic to a local park. To make sure no one strayed on the way to the park, the teachers had the children walk in pairs; as it happens, each pair consisted of a boy and a girl, with all the girls on the left side and all the boys on the right side. Each child wore a T-shirt and shorts in some combination of these colors: blue, green, red, white, and yellow. From the following clues, can you determine the colors of each child's T-shirt and shorts and the order in which the children walked to the park?

1. The children lined up in this order: Alice was first, then the girl in the red T-shirt, the boy in the blue T-shirt, the boy in the blue shorts, and George.

2. No two girls wore the same color T-shirt; no two boys wore the same color T-shirt; no two girls wore the same color shorts; no two boys wore the same color shorts.

3. Two girls (neither of whom was Betty or Jane) wore both green and yellow; neither was paired with the only boy who wore green and yellow (who was not David or Fred). None of the children in green and yellow was first in line, nor was David or Fred.

4. The girl in white shorts was immediately ahead of the boy in white shorts, who was immediately ahead of the girl in the white T-shirt.

5. The girl in red shorts walked with the boy in the red T-shirt, who was not Harry.

6. The girl in the yellow T-shirt walked with the boy in yellow shorts, whose shirt was not blue.

7. Betty, whose partner was not Harry, was ahead of both Carol and Kate.

8. David, whose partner was not Jane, was ahead of Kate.

The solution is on page 156.

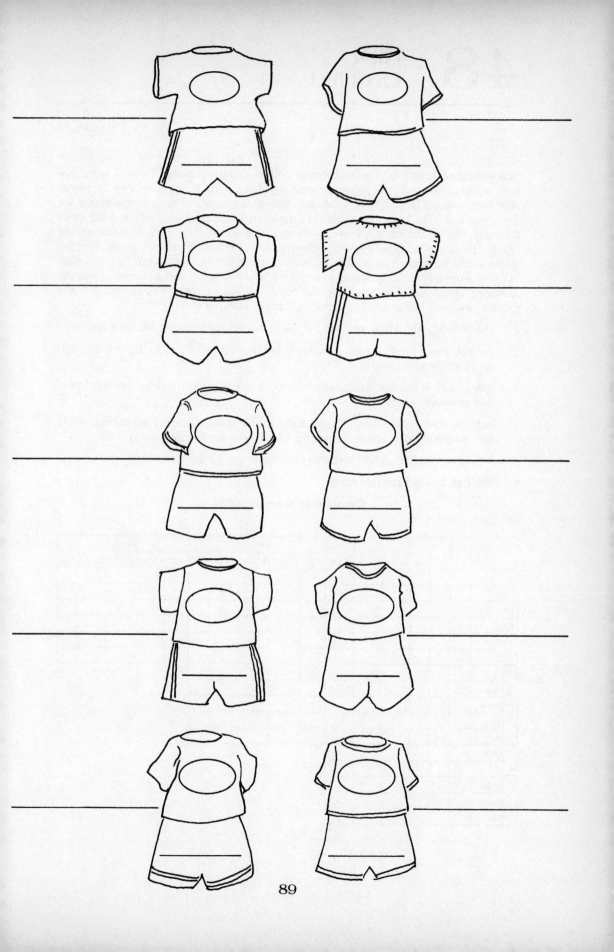

48 RIDE OR HIKE

by W. R. Pinkston

Don and the other five boys in his cabin at Willow Camp had looked forward to the day they would depart from the regular routine and make a trip by horseback to the picnic area atop Lookout Hill for a cookout. By custom, the boys would exchange horses for the return ride. The night before the trip, however, their counselor received the news that only four of the camp's horses were available for the trip, including one named Gizmo. He suggested that two boys volunteer to hike uphill, while four would ride; the hikers would then return on horseback, while two other volunteers would hike downhill to camp. Four boys quickly agreed to be hikers, and the outing was a success. From the following clues, can you determine the boys' full names (one surname is Lee) and exactly how each boy reached, and returned from, Lookout Hill?

1. The Bell boy and Mike were the only ones to exchange mounts for the return trip.

2. The two Rowe brothers were volunteers, but they did not hike together and they did not share the same horse.

3. Ringo, one of the two exchanged mounts, was ridden downhill by the Ward boy; Bob also rode downhill.

4. In preparation for the meal, Greg and the Rowe brothers assisted in cooking, while Bill, who had hiked uphill, helped the Day boy to get the table ready.

5. Joe, who rode Star uphill, hiked downhill with one of the Rowe boys.

6. The Bell boy did not ride Molly.

The solution is on page 156.

	Bell	Day	Lee	Rowe	Rowe	Ward	uphill walk	uphill Gizmo	uphill Molly	uphill Ringo	uphill Star	downhill walk	downhill Gizmo	downhill Molly	downhill Ringo	downhill Star
Bill																
Bob																
Don																
Greg																
Joe																
Mike																
downhill walk																
downhill Gizmo																
downhill Molly																
downhill Ringo																
downhill Star																
uphill walk																
uphill Gizmo																
uphill Molly																
uphill Ringo																
uphill Star																

49 TRAIN RIDE

by Diane Yoko

Bob, Brian, Eileen, Sue, and eight other children rode the train ride at Sunrise Valley's carnival, two children in each of the six cars. The cars were numbered in sequence, and each car was a different color (one was purple). From the following clues, can you deduce the sequence of the car colors, as well as the names of the passengers in each car?

1. Danny's car, which wasn't green, had a higher number than Andy's but a lower number than the blue one.

2. At least one boy rode in the fourth car, which was yellow.

3. Two boys sat in the last car, which was neither blue nor white.

4. The third car wasn't the white one.

5. Laura and another girl sat in the car that immediately followed the green one, which immediately followed the one in which Jane rode.

6. A boy sat with Glen in the second car.

7. Gail sat with her brother.

8. Mary's car, which wasn't the red one or the blue one, immediately followed Paul's.

The solution is on page 157.

50 GEOGRAPHY QUIZ: AFRICA

by Evelyn B. Rosenthal

On a geography quiz, students were given a map of Africa with two cities and three countries identified only by numbers, and the students were asked to name each. The answers of the Quill child and four other students were given in the chart below. From them and the clues which follow, can you find each student's full name and number of right answers?

1. No student was wrong on all five questions, and no two of these five students had the same number right.

2. The Pratt child is not Bob.

3. The Smith child had half as many right as Edna.

4. The Roth child did not have the most right.

5. Both the Pratt child and the Tolbert child had more wrong than the Roth child.

Ann	Khartoum	Tripoli	Ghana	Zambia	Malawi
Bob	Kinshasa	Tripoli	Ghana	Zimbabwe	Mali
Chris	Khartoum	Tunis	Gambia	Zambia	Mali
Dave	Khartoum	Tunis	Ghana	Zaire	Mali
Edna	Kinshasa	Tunis	Gambia	Zambia	Mali

The solution is on page 157.

<table>
<tr><td rowspan="2"></td><td rowspan="2">Pratt</td><td rowspan="2">Quill</td><td rowspan="2">Roth</td><td rowspan="2">Smith</td><td rowspan="2">Tolbert</td><td colspan="5">correct answers</td></tr>
<tr><td>1</td><td>2</td><td>3</td><td>4</td><td>5</td></tr>
<tr><td>Ann</td><td></td><td></td><td></td><td></td><td></td><td></td><td></td><td></td><td></td><td></td></tr>
<tr><td>Bob</td><td></td><td></td><td></td><td></td><td></td><td></td><td></td><td></td><td></td><td></td></tr>
<tr><td>Chris</td><td></td><td></td><td></td><td></td><td></td><td></td><td></td><td></td><td></td><td></td></tr>
<tr><td>Dave</td><td></td><td></td><td></td><td></td><td></td><td></td><td></td><td></td><td></td><td></td></tr>
<tr><td>Edna</td><td></td><td></td><td></td><td></td><td></td><td></td><td></td><td></td><td></td><td></td></tr>
<tr><td rowspan="5">correct answers</td><td>1</td><td></td><td></td><td></td><td></td></tr>
<tr><td>2</td><td></td><td></td><td></td><td></td></tr>
<tr><td>3</td><td></td><td></td><td></td><td></td></tr>
<tr><td>4</td><td></td><td></td><td></td><td></td></tr>
<tr><td>5</td><td></td><td></td><td></td><td></td></tr>
</table>

51 DOGGIE DINNERS

by Dodi Schultz

Charlie, Dave, and five other boys on their block own dogs; at least one of the seven has a dachshund, at least one a fox terrier, and at least one a setter. Each of the dogs has a favorite kind of food and will touch no other brand. From the clues below, can you find what kind of dog each boy owns, each dog's name, and the brand of dog food each likes?

1. John and Sam own the same kind of dog, but the two dogs have different favorite brands: one, Spot, likes Bowwows, the other Meaty Mix.

2. The two collies, neither of which is Billy's, have different favorites; one likes Super Snax, as does Chip, who is neither a setter nor a spaniel.

3. Boots, who is not a spaniel, and Ted's dog, which is not a collie, both like Crumbles.

4. Rover likes Yappies; Ken's dog likes the same brand of dog food as Blackie.

5. The only spaniel on the block, which isn't Sunny, isn't Billy's dog.

6. Sunny, who isn't a setter, likes the same brand as at least one other dog.

7. Skeeter, who isn't a dachshund or a setter, isn't Sam's dog.

8. Only one of the boys gave his dog a name starting with the same letter as his own.

9. Billy's dog is neither Chip nor Sunny.

The solution is on page 157.

owner's name	breed	dog's name	brand
_____	_____	_____	_____
_____	_____	_____	_____
_____	_____	_____	_____
_____	_____	_____	_____
_____	_____	_____	_____
_____	_____	_____	_____
_____	_____	_____	_____

52 THE BUS RIDERS

by Margaret Shoop

Last Friday afternoon, ten workers from the Busy Bee Factory boarded city bus #12 at the corner of Main and 1st streets. The bus, which stops at every corner, proceeds up Main Street, first passing 2nd Street, then 3rd Street, and so on, turning left onto 7th Street, where it first passes Broad Street, then Grand Street, then Capitol Street on its route. From the clues that follow, can you determine where each of the ten workers got off the bus last Friday?

1. Twice as many of the ten workers got off the bus at 7th and Broad as at 7th and Main.

2. None of the ten got off at 2nd and Main or at 3rd and Main.

3. Edwards was the first of the ten workers to leave the bus; none of the others got off when he did or at the next stop.

4. Adams and Carr got off at the same stop; Harris and Innis got off at the same stop.

5. Baker was still on the bus after Davis got off.

6. Grey got off the bus three blocks before Jones got off; Jones got off one stop after French.

7. Harris's stop was not before Adams's stop.

8. Davis didn't get off the bus at Main and 7th, and Baker didn't get off at 7th and Grand.

9. All ten workers had left the bus before it reached 7th and Capitol.

The solution is on page 158.

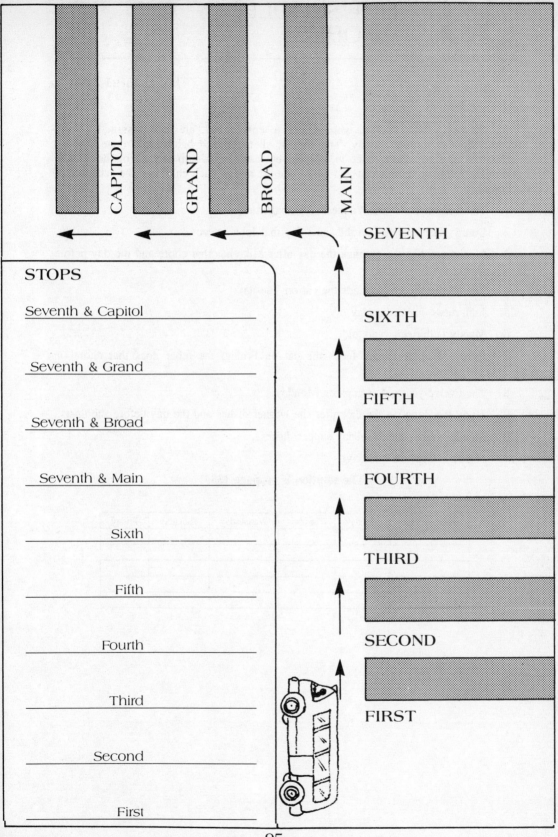

CAPITOL

GRAND

BROAD

MAIN

SEVENTH

SIXTH

FIFTH

FOURTH

THIRD

SECOND

FIRST

STOPS

Seventh & Capitol

Seventh & Grand

Seventh & Broad

Seventh & Main

Sixth

Fifth

Fourth

Third

Second

First

53 HOUSEHOLD CHORES

by Susan Zivich

Mrs. Stewart's five children, who include a ten-year-old, are each assigned a daily chore, Monday through Friday. The chores, all mentioned below, are rotated, so no child has the same chore twice in a week, but each has a turn at each of the chores. From the following clues, can you determine the age of each child and the schedule of chores?

1. The nine-year-old has Wednesday garbage duty.

2. Danny washes dishes on the same day that John sweeps.

3. Mandy empties the garbage the day after Mike has that chore and the day before Danny does it.

4. The fourteen-year-old feeds the cat on Tuesday.

5. John dusts on Wednesday.

6. Mandy is thirteen years old.

7. Either Mike or Danny feeds the cat on Friday; the other does that chore on Thursday.

8. The twelve-year-old sweeps on Monday.

9. Jenny feeds the cat the day after she washes dishes and the day before she dusts.

10. Mandy washes the Thursday supper dishes.

11. Danny sweeps on Tuesday.

The solution is on page 158.

name	age	Monday	Tuesday	Wednesday	Thursday	Friday

54   TOO MUCH OF A GOOD THING

by Julie Spence

Sometimes we all experience too much of a good thing; last Tuesday, such was the case in different ways for Shannon and four of her friends. One of the five went shopping at money-saving sales and spent too much of her allotted budget, making things a little tight until payday. From the clues below, can you determine each woman's full name (one surname is Sukow), age and what good thing she experienced too much of? (Note: All ages are expressed in whole numbers, and no two of the five are the same age.)

1. Ms. Marcott is two years older than the one who pulled a muscle overexercising and three years older than Tracy, who is not Ms. Farrell.

2. The one who stayed up too late reading and consequently overslept the next morning is not twenty-three years old.

3. Mandy is one year younger than Ms. Wilson and two years older than the one who stayed at the beach too long and got a bad sunburn.

4. Amy is older than Ms. Farrell, who is twenty-two years old.

5. The one who ate too much pizza and ruined her diet is a year older than Ms. Rogers and two years younger than Nikki.

The solution is on page 159.

	Farrell	Marcott	Rogers	Sukow	Wilson	exercise	pizza	read	spent	sun	ages		
Amy													
Mandy													
Nikki													
Shannon													
Tracy													
ages													
exercise					
pizza					
read					
spent					
sun					

55 CAREFREE CRUISING

by Frank A. Bauckman

Last January, five couples—the Larsens, the Millers, the Norrises, the Olsens, and the Parkers, each hailing from a different northeastern state—met on a Caribbean cruise, and became good friends during their two weeks aboard the *Carefree*. By coincidence, all five women—one of whom is named Peggy—are registered nurses, and so found immediately that they had much in common; Lew and the other men of the group all follow different pursuits—variously, accounting, banking, law, medicine, or stock brokerage. From the clues below, try to determine the full name of each couple, where each came from, and each husband's occupation.

1. Ken and Una's husband—neither of whom is a broker—enjoyed competing at shuffleboard against the team of Larsen and the man from Pennsylvania.

2. Ken is not a banker, and is not Rose's husband; Jack, who is not Toni's husband, is not from New Jersey; Norris is not a broker.

3. When the five wives—Sue and Mrs. Parker and the accountant's wife and the woman from New York and Ned's wife—got talking, they found to their surprise that all had been married in the very same year.

4. Sue is neither Mrs. Larsen nor the doctor's wife; Rose is neither Mrs. Parker nor the accountant's wife.

5. All five wives—Mrs. Larsen and Rose and Ned's wife and the doctor's wife and the woman from Connecticut—spent many hours in the ship's pool.

6. The banker and Mel—neither of whose last name is Miller—found they had attended the same New England college; Una's husband and the man from Maryland had both attended schools in the Middle West.

The solution is on page 159.

The chart, although divided because of its size, is used in the normal way.

	Peggy	Rose	Sue	Toni	Una	Larsen	Miller	Norris	Olsen	Parker	acc't.	bank.	law.	doc.	broker
Jack															
Ken															
Lew															
Mel															
Ned															
Conn.															
Md.															
N.J.															
N.Y.															
Pa.															
acc't.															
bank.															
law.															
doc.															
broker															
Larsen															
Miller															
Norris															
Olsen															
Parker															

	Conn.	Md.	N.J.	N.Y.	Pa.
Jack					
Ken					
Lew					
Mel					
Ned					

56 ICE DANCING

by Cheryl L. McLaughlin

Ten male-female couples, who included a woman named Clara, participated in the ice-dancing competition at the Westwood Winter Fair. Each contestant wore the same color as his or her partner; one couple wore green. From the following clues, can you determine each couple's full names (one man's surname is McMann, and one woman's is Ellis) and costume color, as well as the order in which the ten couples were ranked in the competition?

1. Jack Peters and his partner wore black and finished in first place; Ann and her partner, who wasn't Frank, wore yellow and placed second; Ms. Kent and her partner placed third; Henry and his partner, Ms. Land, placed fourth; Mr. Stark and his partner placed fifth.

2. Diana and her partner, Mr. Drake, placed directly ahead of the couple whose costumes were pink, who placed directly ahead of Bob and his partner, Ms. Hardin.

3. Mr. Benet and his partner placed directly behind Dee and her partner and directly ahead of Mr. Ulman and his partner, Wendy, who wore purple.

4. Jim and his partner, who wasn't Ann, placed directly ahead of Mr. Adams and his partner (whose costumes were neither the blue ones nor the white ones), who placed directly ahead of Mike and his partner, Ms. Quinn, whose costumes were orange.

5. Ms. Frost and her partner placed eighth; Mr. Nash and his partner, who wasn't Gina, placed ninth; Wayne and his partner Gwen, in gray costumes, placed tenth.

6. Tom and his partner, Ms. Clark, placed directly ahead of Bill and his partner, whose costumes were red and who finished two places ahead of Mary and her partner; Mary is not Ms. Thomas.

7. Tim and his partner, Ms. Jacobs, whose costumes weren't blue, placed directly ahead of Mr. Ryan and his partner, Ms. Inness.

8. Cathy, who is not Ms. Thomas and was not Mr. Olsen's partner, placed ahead of Nancy, whose costume wasn't white.

The solution is on page 160.

	men			women		color
1st place	_____	_____	&	_____	_____	_____
2nd place	_____	_____	&	_____	_____	_____
3rd place	_____	_____	&	_____	_____	_____
4th place	_____	_____	&	_____	_____	_____
5th place	_____	_____	&	_____	_____	_____
6th place	_____	_____	&	_____	_____	_____
7th place	_____	_____	&	_____	_____	_____
8th place	_____	_____	&	_____	_____	_____
9th place	_____	_____	&	_____	_____	_____
10th place	_____	_____	&	_____	_____	_____

57 LICENSE PLATES AND BARNS

by Evelyn B. Rosenthal

A family of five, motoring through New England, added interest to the trip by seeing how many out-of-state license plates and how many red barns each could spot. From the following clues, can you identify the family members and find how many license plates and barns each saw?

1. The largest number of license plates seen by any one person is one more than the largest number of barns seen by any one person.

2. Chris did not see the fewest barns.

3. The boy saw three more license plates than Gert did.

4. The five different numbers of license plates seen are consecutive; so are the five different numbers of barns.

5. Since the parents took turns driving and had to watch the road, together they saw one more license plate than the girls together but fewer barns than the girls together.

6. Lou saw more license plates than Kit, who saw the same number of license plates and barns.

7. Everyone saw at least one barn, and one person saw only one.

8. Lee saw two more license plates than one of the girls did.

9. The boy saw the same number of license plates as he saw barns.

10. Chris saw more license plates than Lee did.

The solution is on page 160.

Use this space for solving.

58 THE EXIT POLL

by Ellen K. Rodehorst

One recent election day, a local television station sent reporters to the five voting districts in town to poll voters as they left the voting booths. The mayoral race between incumbent Perry and his rival Roberts promised to be close, and an important bond issue was also on the ballot. The interviews with Diane, Mel, and three others, each from a different voting district, were chosen for showing on the air after the polls closed. From the clues below, can you determine the full name of the interviewee selected from each district (one surname is Carson) and his or her vote for mayor and decision on the bond issue?

1. The voter from the first district, who is not Sam, voted for the less popular mayoral candidate among the five interviewees.

2. Mr. Bailey and the woman from the fifth district made totally untrue statements to the reporters, while the other three told the truth.

3. Ann, who is not voter West, said, "I don't like Roberts, so I voted for Perry."

4. Tom, who is not the first-district voter, told the reporter, "I voted for Perry and against the bond issue."

5. Ms. Knox, who is not the female voter from the third district, said, "I voted for Roberts and yes on the bond issue."

6. Mr. Greer, who is not the second-district voter, said, "I voted for Perry."

7. Among these five voters, only one voted no on the bond issue.

The solution is on page 161.

district	first name	last name	for Perry	for Roberts	bond issue	
1					yes	no
2					yes	no
3					yes	no
4					yes	no
5					yes	no

59 THE SOFTBALL GAME

by Margaret Shoop

In the championship game of a church softball league, the Trinity Arrows played the St. Mark's Braves; the game was limited to seven innings. From the clues which follow, can you determine the number of runs scored by each team in each inning?

1. A home run in the bottom of the seventh inning clinched the game for the Braves, who won 8–7; that home run gave the Braves the distinction of having scored the most runs in one inning of play.

2. In four innings, both teams scored.

3. In two innings, neither team scored.

4. The score was tied at the end of the third, fourth, and sixth innings; at the end of the fourth inning, the score was 2–2.

5. The score was not tied at the end of the second inning.

6. The Arrows scored in five innings.

7. At least one team scored in the second inning.

8. At the end of the fifth inning, the Arrows were ahead; they had not been leading at the end of any prior inning.

The solution is on page 161.

inning	1	2	3	4	5	6	7	total
Arrows								
Braves								

60 HALLOWEEN TREAT

by Randall L. Whipkey

As an extra treat for trick-or-treaters this past Halloween, the five couples who live on one side of one block of Summerset Street—their houses, from one end of the block to the other, are numbered 101, 103, 105, 107, and 109—dressed up in costumes and decorated their foyers, each couple choosing a different theme. From the clues below, can you deduce the full names of each couple (one woman is Monica), their house number, and the theme each used?

1. The Drakes' theme was neither "Dracula's Castle" nor "Ye Olde Graveyarde."

2. Larry and Linda are not husband and wife.

3. Mike's house is between Nora's and that of the couple whose theme was "Ye Olde Graveyarde."

4. John isn't Mr. Drake.

5. The Colemans live next door to Linda and her husband.

6. Kevin's house is between those of Mr. and Mrs. English and the couple whose theme was "Dracula's Castle," neither of whose address is 101.

7. Mr. and Mrs. Bowers live next door to the couple whose theme was "Invaders from Space."

8. Neither John and his wife nor Larry and his had "Ye Olde Graveyarde" as a theme.

9. Nick's house is between those of Kristi and her husband and the Drakes, neither of whom lives at Number 103.

10. Nora and her husband don't live at Number 109.

11. Mike's wife isn't Kristi.

12. Kristi isn't Mrs. Coleman.

13. The Colemans' theme wasn't "Invaders from Space."

14. The Austins live next door to the couple whose theme was "African Safari."

15. Joan and her husband did not choose "The Ghost House" as their theme.

16. Linda isn't Mrs. English.

The solution is on page 162.

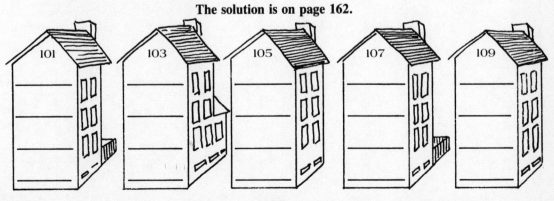

61 CAT ANTICS

by Mary A. Powell

When Judy moved with her cat to the Gramercy Towers apartment building, she was delighted to find George and four other cat owners already living there. As typical cat owners, the six like to tell one another about their pets' latest tricks and pranks; one cat retrieves toy mice and brings them back to its owner to throw again and again. From the following clues, can you find the full name of each owner, the name of each person's cat, its latest antic, and the floor on which each lives?

1. There are six floors in the apartment building. Helen and Mr. King, who both have black cats, live on the same floor. Pixie, a tawny Abyssinian, lives on the same floor as the cat (which is not black) that dips milk from a glass with its paw.

2. Susan lives two floors above Larry, who lives three floors above Price, who is not Helen.

3. The black Scamper is not the cat that opens cupboard doors and knocks the contents to the floor.

4. The cat that walks on the tops of doors lives on a higher floor than the white cat named Little Bit, but below Ms. Blake, who is not Susan.

5. Brad lives two floors above the cat that sleeps on its back and three floors below the cat (which is not Pixie) that hoards its treasures (wool yarn, bits of paper, and old socks) under the bedspread.

6. The orange-and-white cat that belongs to Davis is not Tinker Bell, who does not belong to King.

7. Adams lives more than one floor below Evans.

8. Pixie, who lives with a woman, is too dignified to sleep on his back.

9. Brad's cat is not Fuzzy and is not the cat that prances across door tops.

10. Grayling was named for his color.

The solution is on page 162.

Gramercy Towers

6th floor	
5th floor	
4th floor	
3rd floor	
2nd floor	
1st floor	

62 IMMIGRANT ENTREPRENEURS

by Tara Lynn Fulton

Over the last twenty years, Smith and four other men from different countries each opened a business in one of the five boroughs of New York City; one is a dry cleaner. From the clues given below, can you determine each man's native country (one came from Greece), business, and location, as well as the order in which the five businesses were opened? (The names of the immigrants have all been Anglicized.)

1. The dress shop is not the business in Brooklyn or Manhattan.

2. The dress shop was opened just after the business in Queens.

3. Neither the man from Poland nor the owner of the Queens business sells food.

4. Miller's business, which wasn't the first to open, opened just before the fruit stand.

5. Allen is neither the immigrant from Ireland nor the one from Italy.

6. Marshall and the owner of the Bronx business are from Italy and Greece.

7. The first business to be opened was the restaurant; the last was the one in Manhattan.

8. The deli is owned by the man from Germany.

9. Brown's business is on Staten Island.

10. Marshall was not the last of the five to open his business.

The solution is on page 163.

Use the split chart in the same way as a regular solving chart.

	deli	dress	dry cl.	fruit	rest.	Ger.	Gr.	Ire.	It.	Pol.	Bklyn.	Bx.	Man.	Qns.	S.I.
Allen															
Brown															
Marshall															
Miller															
Smith															
1															
2															
3															
4															
5															
Bklyn.															
Bx.															
Man.															
Qns.															
S.I.															
Ger.															
Gr.															
Ire.															
It.															
Pol.															

	1	2	3	4	5
Allen					
Brown					
Marshall					
Miller					
Smith					

63 NEWSPAPER DROPS

by Julie Spence

Every day, Paul Kelly drops off bundles of the *Cosmopolis Star* in Ellsworth and four other small towns just outside the city. The papers are dropped at five different kinds of business establishments; in one town, they are delivered to a grocery. Last Tuesday, Paul was ill, so he asked his cousin Mike to drop off the papers for him. Paul gave Mike a list indicating where in each town he should drop off the papers, but unfortunately, Mike lost the list; although he remembered the five kinds of businesses, he *mis*remembered which was in what town. The result was that in each of the first four towns in which he stopped, he went to the wrong place and was then directed to the correct drop-off place. Since Mike knew there was only one drop-off place of each type, once he had dropped a bundle of papers at a correct place, he did not mistakenly stop at that same type of place in a subsequent town. From the clues below, can you determine the order in which Mike made the drops in the five towns, the population of each town (all are different), the place he mistakenly went first, and the correct drop-off place in each?

1. One place Mike went to by mistake was a drugstore.

2. In one town, Mike first went to the bakery and was sent to the hardware store.

3. Elmwood, population 1,200, is the largest of the five towns; one of the others has half its population.

4. In Prescott, which has a population of 800, Mike went to the dry cleaner's by mistake.

5. In one town, Mike first stopped at the hardware store and was sent to the drugstore.

6. Woodville, which doesn't have a bakery and wasn't Mike's last stop, has twice the population of Mike's first stop.

7. Hudson, which doesn't have a dry cleaner's, isn't the smallest town with a population of 500.

The solution is on page 163.

Use this space for solving.

64 THE CHEERLEADERS

by Evelyn B. Rosenthal

Judy and four other girls are cheerleaders at the Field School. Each girl has a different one of the letters of the school's name on her uniform sweater. No two of the five are the same height or the same weight. From the following clues, can you find each girl's full name (one surname is Howard), height, weight, and the letter she has on her sweater?

1. The girls are two pounds apart in weight and one inch apart in height.

2. The shortest girl is lighter than Mona and heavier than the North girl.

3. The Garner girl, who does not have the *E*, weighs less than Kay and more than the girl with the *L*.

4. Lila weighs most but is shorter than the Murray girl.

5. The Fuller girl is shorter than the girl with the *I* and taller than Ilene, who does not have the *L*.

6. The girl with the *E* is the tallest, 5'6"; the one with the *F* is the lightest, 103 pounds.

The solution is on page 164.

The solution is on page 164.

	F	I	E	L	D
first name					
last name					
height					
weight					

65 WHERE DO THE TREES GO?

by Dodi Schultz

Arbor Drive is an east-west street just one block long, with ten houses on each side; the houses on the north side are odd-numbered 1 to 19 (west to east), those opposite on the south side 2 to 20. Despite its name, the street was treeless until the Acme Tree Service arrived with a truckload of ten young trees, including a birch. The workmen were presented with the names of the twenty families and advised that a tree was to be planted in front of every other house, in accord with the clues below. They figured out not only where to plant the trees, but exactly who lives where. Can you do the same? *(Note: "East" and "west" do not necessarily mean on the same side of the street.)*

1. The Elgins and the Fosters live on the south side; the beech and the sycamore are to go on the north side.

2. The Ingersolls live on the same side as the Todds.

3. The Hills live immediately between the Baers and the Jacksons, who live directly opposite the sophora-planting site.

4. The ailanthus is to be planted west of the beech and directly opposite the Quinns' home.

5. The Kayes live west of the Ingersolls; both families live on the south side.

6. The Fosters and the Garners live as far apart as possible, as do the Kayes and the Landmans.

7. The Todds live east of the Millers and west of the Aldens.

8. The Ryans live immediately between the O'Neills and the Parkers; the linden is to be planted directly opposite the Parkers' house.

9. One family's name begins with the same letter as the kind of tree which is to go in front of its home.

10. The flowering pear is to be planted directly opposite the Todds' home; no tree is to be planted directly across from the Nivens' house.

11. No tree is to be planted in front of the Sommers' home, which is on the side of the street where the oak is to go; the Todds live on the other side.

12. The Baers, the Carters, and the Danes all live on the north side.

13. The sophora, which is not to go in front of the Ryans' home, is to be planted east of the flowering pear.

14. The O'Neills live west of the Nivens, who live on the north side.

15. No tree is to be planted in front of the Landmans' house.

16. The Quinns live east of the Millers and west of the Ryans.

17. Neither the sycamore nor the ginkgo is to be planted in front of an end house.

18. The elm is to go in front of the house next to the Millers, who live west of the Carters.

19. No tree is to be planted directly opposite another tree.

The solution is on page 164.

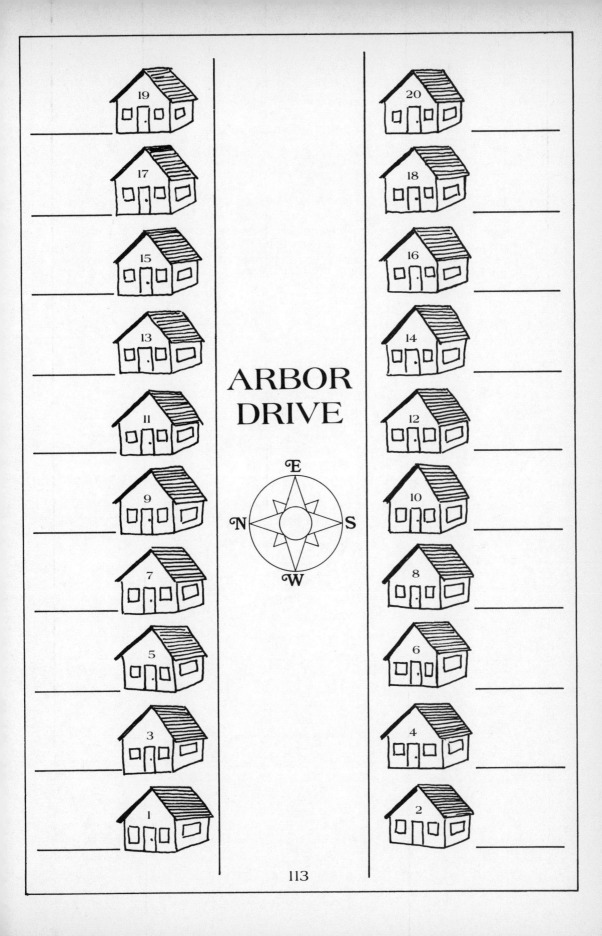

ARBOR DRIVE

CHALLENGER

66 THE DOUGHNUT SHOP

by Nancy R. Patterson

During lunch hour last Thursday, Mr. Bond and five other customers of the Doughnut Shop each bought a different number of doughnuts, choosing among four flavors available (one flavor was sugar raised). From the following clues, can you deduce how many doughnuts of each flavor each customer purchased?

1. Mr. Drake's order was twice as large as the order for half cinnamon doughnuts and half lemon doughnuts.

2. The six customers bought two dozen doughnuts altogether.

3. The order for half cinnamon doughnuts and half chocolate doughnuts was exactly three times as large as one of the other orders.

4. Ms. Austin bought three different flavors.

5. Ms. Fox bought twice as many doughnuts as Mr. Ewell.

6. No two orders combined any of the same flavors—for example, if one order included both chocolate and lemon, no other order included both; nor did any two orders include the same quantity of any flavor.

7. The largest order did not include more than four doughnuts of any one flavor.

8. Ms. Clark, who ordered no lemon doughnuts, bought half as many doughnuts as the customer who ordered chocolate doughnuts only.

The solution is on page 165.

Use this space for solving.

67 THE BIG CLEANUP

by Mary A. Powell

Five women decided that they would pool their surplus treasures and hold a neighborhood sale after taking five weeks to clean out closets, kitchen cupboards, basements, attics, and garages. From the following clues, can you determine the full name of each woman and the week she performed each task?

1. No woman attacked more than one area in any week, and no more than two women chose the same task in any week.

2. Brenda and Ms. Davis chose identical jobs for three consecutive weeks.

3. Doris and Ms. Adams chose identical jobs the second week.

4. No basements were cleaned out the fifth week, no attics were cleaned out the fourth week, and no garages were cleaned out the second week.

5. Celia and Ms. Bates cleaned out their kitchen cupboards before the other three did; Evelyn and Ms. Evans cleaned out their basements before the other three did; Ms. Collins cleaned out her attic the second week. *(Note: All five women are mentioned here.)*

6. Amanda and Ms. Evans chose no identical tasks in any week, but Amanda and Evelyn chose identical jobs during both of the last two weeks.

7. The woman whose first and last names begin with the same letter was the only one who cleaned out her kitchen cupboards the first week.

8. Doris cleaned out her garage before she cleaned out her basement.

9. Ms. Collins cleaned out her garage before Ms. Bates cleaned out her attic.

The solution is on page 166.

first name last name					
1st week					
2nd week					
3rd week					
4th week					
5th week					

68 MUDVILLE'S MARCHING BAND

by Julie Spence

The Mudville High School Marching Band consists of seven rows. Tom and six other students march in different rows and play different instruments. From the following clues, can you determine each student's full name, instrument, and row?

1. Schubert, who is not the one who plays trombone, marches farther back than Smith.

2. The boy who plays the drum marches in the middle row.

3. The trumpet player marches just ahead of Sam, who is ahead of Faulkner.

4. There are no trombones in the last row.

5. Judy doesn't march in the first or last row.

6. Brian, whose last name is not Miller, does not march in the last row and is not the trumpeter.

7. The flute player is ahead, but not just ahead of Faye, who is ahead of the Billings girl.

8. Both the saxophone player and Miller are ahead of Jilk, who is not the one who plays tuba.

9. Max marches just behind the Truman girl and just ahead of the clarinet player.

10. Susan doesn't march in the last row.

The solution is on page 166.

ROW	NAME	INSTRUMENT
1	_____	_____
2	_____	_____
3	_____	_____
4	_____	_____
5	_____	_____
6	_____	_____
7	_____	_____

69 ENGLISH AND MATH SCHEDULES

by Margaret Shoop

Ken and four other young people are all enrolled in English 101 and Math 101 at the same community college. From the clues that follow, can you determine each student's full name (one last name is Collins) and when each has English and math?

1. All classes at the college begin on the hour and last fifty minutes; the first period begins at 8:00 A.M.

2. All five students have finished both their English and math classes by 1:50 P.M., and each has English and math in consecutive periods, in one order or the other; no two of the five have English or math at the same time.

3. None of the five has English at 1:00 P.M.

4. The only one of the women who has an 8:00 A.M. English or math class meets Abernathy in the college coffee shop each school day at 10:15 A.M.

5. Dalton has math class during the period after Lauren has it.

6. Jim, whose last name isn't Dalton, has English while Butler has math and has math while Butler has English.

7. Before Elliott has gone to either English or math class, Nick has finished both.

8. Michelle, whose last name isn't Butler and who has English before math, has finished both classes by 11:50.

The solution is on page 167.

STUDENT					
8:00					
9:00					
10:00					
11:00					
12:00					
1:00					

70 THE AUCTION

by Randall L. Whipkey

One item offered in this year's Summerset Hospital Benefit Auction was an all-expenses-paid weekend for two in Atlantic City. Four different bidders, including Baker, participated in the bidding for the trip. From the following clues, can you deduce each bidder's full name, the sequence in which the four bid, and the amount of each bid?

1. The starting bid was $25, and the tenth and final bid was $400.

2. Case's third bid was four times as much as Adams's first bid.

3. Ian bid a second time immediately before Ms. Davis entered the auction.

4. Karen made the eighth bid.

5. Case once raised the previous bid $50.

6. Linda and Karen made different numbers of bids.

7. Ian's third bid was three times as much as Jim's second bid.

8. Karen once followed Case in the bidding with a $50 raise.

9. Jim's second bid was four times as much as his first bid.

10. At no time did a bidder follow a raise of his or her bid with the next bid.

11. Ian's second bid was for $75 more than his first.

12. The minimum raise in the auction was $25.

13. Neither woman raised immediately following the other's bid.

The solution is on page 168.

124

BID	BIDDER	AMOUNT
1	_____	_____
2	_____	_____
3	_____	_____
4	_____	_____
5	_____	_____
6	_____	_____
7	_____	_____
8	_____	_____
9	_____	_____
10	_____	_____

71 ART CLASSES

by Ellen K. Rodehorst

Ms. Potter, an elementary-school art teacher, teaches seven grades, kindergarten through sixth. Each grade meets for art class at least twice during the school week (Monday through Friday), always in the same period. The school day consists of six class periods, three in the morning and three in the afternoon, with a lunch hour between; Ms. Potter has at least one period free each day. Currently, each grade is concentrating on a particular medium or project; one is working with clay. From the clues below, can you find each grade's art-class schedule and special project?

1. The sixth-graders are not the ones doing block printing.

2. The first-graders do not go to art class on Wednesday.

3. On Friday afternoon, the class that does block printing meets after one of Ms. Potter's free periods and before the fifth-grade class, which is not the group doing montages.

4. A kindergarten art class meets on Monday.

5. On Tuesday, the second-graders, who are not doing acrylic painting, come to class just after Ms. Potter's first class of the day and just before the lunch break.

6. Ms. Potter has more classes in third period than in any other period and more classes on Wednesday than on any other day.

7. Both the class that works with acrylic paints and the fourth-graders have art classes on Tuesday, Wednesday, and Thursday only.

8. Fifth period on Tuesday is not a free period for Ms. Potter.

9. The class that works on weaving meets on Tuesday, Thursday, and Friday only.

10. Ms. Potter teaches finger painting to one of her Tuesday classes.

11. The class that is doing watercolors meets only twice a week; the sixth-grade class meets four times a week; all the other classes meet three times a week.

12. The third-graders do not have art class in the fourth period.

The solution is on page 169.

PERIOD	MON.	TUES.	WED.	THURS.	FRI.
1st					
2nd					
3rd					
LUNCH					
4th					
5th					
6th					

72 HOUSE PAINT

by Mary A. Powell

Zionsburg is an old city in which most of the houses have been painted white for nearly a century, but this year things have changed. In one block on Oak Street, the owners of the ten houses—five married couples and five single people—decided to repaint. At the end of the painting spree, only two of the houses were still white, and they sported colorful trim. The houses on the block are numbered from west to east—1 through 9 on the north side, 2 through 10 on the south side—as shown in the accompanying diagram. From the following clues, can you find the full name(s) of the owner(s) of each house (one last name is Granger), the current basic color, and the trim color?

1. Susan lives next door to the Harmon house; Rosa lives next door to the Lyons house.

2. Tom, whose house has red trim, and the Evans couple, who do not live in number 2, live as far apart as possible.

3. Each husband's first name begins with the same letter as his wife's first name.

4. Three houses have red trim, four have white trim, two have blue trim, and one beige house has brown trim; no two houses have identical basic-and-trim-color combinations.

5. These five houses are on the north side (in no particular order): Tanya's, a green house, number 3, the DeWitt house, and the Forrest house, which is yellow.

6. These five houses are on the south side (in no particular order): the Carter house, Mark's and Marie's house, number 8, and two houses painted with both white and blue.

7. Paul, who lives on the north side of the block, is the only person who lives between two single people; Peter is the only person who lives between two married couples.

8. The yellow house on the south side is directly across the street from a beige house, as is the yellow house on the north side.

9. When Sam ran out of trim paint, he borrowed some from his next-door neighbor, Karen. When Pamela ran out of trim paint, she borrowed some from her next-door neighbor, Ned. (Note: Basic house paint and trim paint are not interchangeable.)

10. The Jones house is directly across the street from the gray house, which is next door to the Bentley house.

11. The single women chose the same basic color; the single men chose the same trim color.

12. Nora and Adams live directly across the street from each other, in houses with the same basic color; Ken and his wife live directly across the street from Russell and his wife, in houses with the same trim color.

13. One house is brown.

The solution is on page 169.

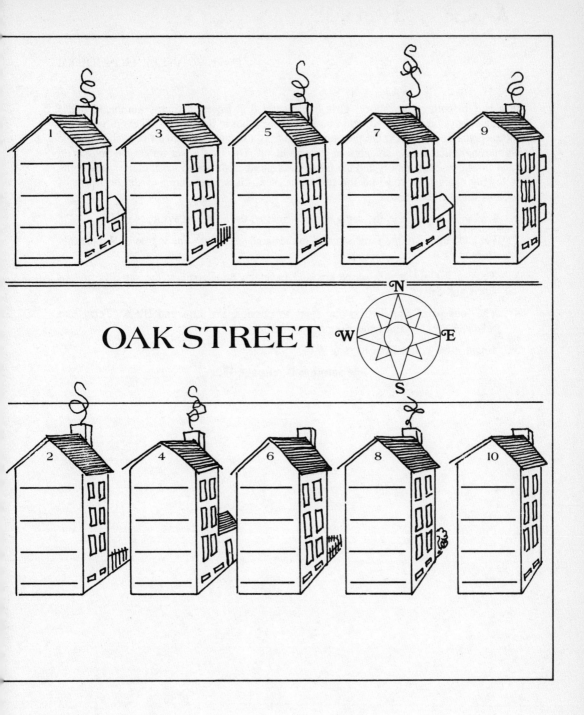

OAK STREET

73 STUDENTS' ROOMS

by Evelyn B. Rosenthal

In a certain college dormitory, girls live on the first floor, in rooms numbered under #20, and boys on the second; odd-numbered rooms house freshmen, and even-numbered rooms house sophomores. On the opposite page is a layout of the two floors showing the eight rooms that house students in this problem. The two lower-numbered rooms on each floor house art majors and the two higher-numbered rooms, math majors. From the following clues, can you find the full name, sex, class, and major of the occupant of each of these eight rooms?

1. Lee and Gray live in the same vertical line; so do Fran and White.

2. Pat and Green are the same sex and in the same year; the same is true of Ronnie and Brown.

3. Terry and Gold are the same sex and have the same majors; the same is true of Chris and Silver.

4. The four pairs who live as far apart as possible are Lou and Black, Terry and Silver, Kim and Blue, and Ronnie and White.

5. Green, who is not Lou, lives in #14.

The solution is on page 170.

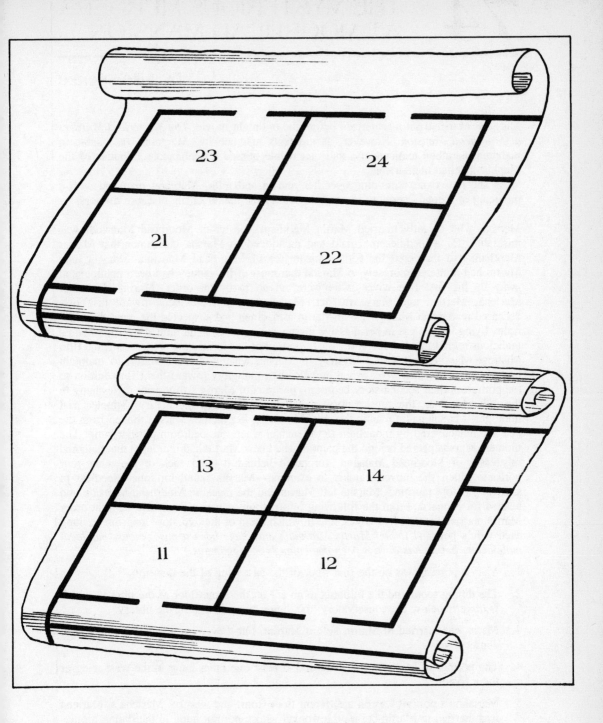

74 THE MYSTERIOUS MURDERS AT MOORHEAD MANSION

by Julie Spence

Margaret Marshall sat mesmerized before the midnight movie, *The Mysterious Murders at Moorhead Mansion*. However, as moments marched by, Margaret was unable to maintain marathon meticulosity, and meanwhile missed miscellaneous minutiae of the Mephistophelian melodrama.

As she mused next morning over her muffin and milk, Margaret managed with a modicum of mental energy to remember most of the matter of the macabre mystery.

Marsha, who recently married Martin Markham, master of Moorhead Mansion, was miserable, for a meddlesome maid had mentioned to Marsha the rumor that Master Markham had murdered the former mistresses of Moorhead Mansion. Many a time Martin had muttered morosely to Marsha that most of his money had been manipulated away by his first five wives, who were, in no particular order, Maria, Marianne, Marlena, Martha, and Mary. In fact, Martin was so malevolent toward his now-deceased mates that Marsha feared Martin a madman and suspected the maid might be right. Lying motionless in her massive master bedroom, Marsha mulled over the maid's malicious remarks and stared at the misty portrait of her immediate predecessor, the fifth Mistress Markham. It was a mystery to Marsha what motivated Martin to maintain portraits of his former wives when he held such malignity toward them. In addition to the portrait in their second-story bedroom, portraits of Martin's four prior mates hung in the billiards room, the conservatory, the dining room, and the library. Minutes past midnight, Marsha had a mantic thought. Mustering her mettle, Marsha moved from the bed and maneuvered by moonlight to the mantel where the bedroom portrait hung. The moment Marsha peered behind the painting she knew Martin had murdered the maligned mistresses of Moorhead Mansion, for taped behind it—and each of the other four portraits which she moved quickly to examine—Marsha found millions. Needless to say, long before morning, Marsha left Martin and the macabre Moorhead Mansion and headed for Monaco. From the following information, can you determine in what order Martin married his first five wives, and in which room of the two-story mansion he hung each wife's portrait? *(Note: Martin Markham may have been a misogynous, maniacal malefactor, but he has always been meticulously monogamous.)*

1. Mary's portrait was on the first floor of the east wing of the mansion.

2. The dining room and the billiards room are on the same floor as the library, which is *directly* below the conservatory; the dining room is east of the library.

3. Maria was married to Martin before Martha, but they were not married to Martin consecutively.

4. The portrait of Martin's first wife and at least one other hung in the west wing of the mansion.

5. Marianne's portrait was on a different floor from, and west of, Marlena's; Marlena was married to Martin before the woman whose portrait hung in the dining room.

6. Mary and the woman whose portrait hung in the dining room were not married to Martin consecutively.

The solution is on page 171.

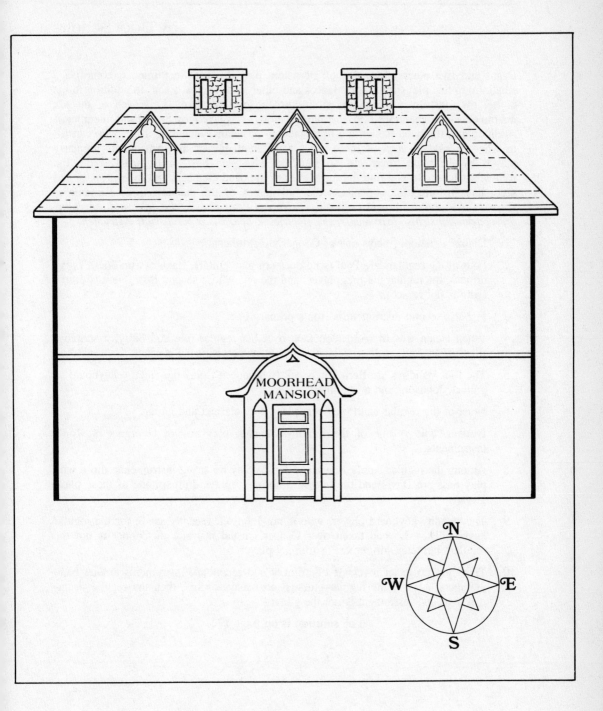

75 MUSICAL CHAIRS

Evans and five other musicians, all of whom play different instruments, comprise a small group that plays for school dances and other local events. Each, in addition to his or her own instrument, can also sit in for one of the others (i.e., each of the six instruments—all mentioned in the clues below—is played by two band members). Additionally, the band has on tap four standby musicians, including Tom, who can fill in when necessary; each of these plays a different one of the instruments regularly played by the band (there are no standbys who play bass or trumpet). From the following clues, can you find the full names of the band members and their primary and secondary instruments, as well as the full names of the standbys (one surname is Gibbons) and the instrument each plays? *(Note: In this puzzle, the bass and the guitar are considered string instruments; the electric keyboard is a percussion instrument.)*

1. Diana, a standby, plays one of Cooper's instruments.

2. Four of the regulars are Paul (who does not play guitar), Baxter (who doesn't play drums), the regular clarinet player, and the one whose second instrument is drums (who is not Janice).

3. Fisher's second instrument is Ron's primary one.

4. When Helen was ill, Anderson took over her regular role and Sally, a standby, filled in on Anderson's regular instrument, which isn't the clarinet.

5. The four standbys are Ben, Hitchcock (who doesn't play the electric keyboard or guitar), Johnson, and a drummer.

6. None of the regular band members plays both clarinet and guitar.

7. Iverson, who is one of the standbys, cannot play any of George's or Ron's instruments.

8. Among the regulars, only Frank and Janice play no string instruments; those who play bass are Davis and the one who normally plays drums; none of these plays guitar.

9. The standby keyboard player, who is not Johnson, recently sat in for the regular keyboardist, who had taken over Cooper's usual instrument; Cooper is not the regular clarinetist, drummer, or trumpet player.

10. There are no exact reversals of primary and secondary instruments among band members; e.g., if the regular guitarist also plays drums, then the regular drummer's second instrument is not the guitar.

The solution is on page 172.

REGULARS

first name	last name	primary instrument	secondary instrument
_____	_____	_____	_____
_____	_____	_____	_____
_____	_____	_____	_____
_____	_____	_____	_____
_____	_____	_____	_____
_____	_____	_____	_____

STANDBYS

_____	_____	_____
_____	_____	_____
_____	_____	_____
_____	_____	_____

SOLUTIONS

1. CERAMICS PIECES

Caroline was the first to finish (clue 2). Since Maxine finished her masterpiece before the ashtray (clue 3), and the ashtray was finished before the fruit dish and Frieda's project (clue 1), Maxine was second, and the other pieces were finished third, fourth, and fifth, respectively. Frieda must have made the candlesticks (clue 3). Caroline didn't make the planter (clue 2), so she made the poodle statue and Maxine made the planter. Evelyn didn't make the ashtray (clue 3), so Brenda did, and Evelyn made the fruit dish. In summary, in order of completion:

> Caroline, poodle statue
> Maxine, planter
> Brenda, ashtray
> Evelyn, fruit dish
> Frieda, candlesticks

2. THE MARATHON

Michael was the winner of the race, and Kenny was second (lines 23–25). Kenny's last name is Lane (line 18). Polly came in fifth (lines 15–16). Joe came in third (lines 27–28) and Lou, by elimination, finished fourth. The last name of the winner, Michael, isn't Zinner (lines 13–14), Byrd (line 26), or Jensen (lines 19–20); it is therefore North. Mr. Zinner can't be Polly, and since he didn't finish third (line 17), he's not Joe (lines 27–28), so he's Lou. Joe isn't Byrd (lines 26–27), so he's Jensen, and Polly is Byrd. In sum:

> 1st, Michael North
> 2nd, Kenny Lane
> 3rd, Joe Jensen
> 4th, Lou Zinner
> 5th, Polly Byrd

3. THE ACCOUNTING DEPARTMENT

Brenda's last name is not Stanley or Taylor (clue 2), nor Underwood (clue 5); she is Brenda Reese. The Internal Auditor is not Anna or Brenda (clue 4), or Dora (clue 6), so Connie is the Internal Auditor. Connie's last name is not Taylor (clue 1) or Underwood (clue 5); she must be Connie Stanley. The woman who worked in Accounts Payable is neither Brenda Reese nor Ms. Underwood (clue 5), so she is Ms. Taylor. Her first name is not Dora (clue 3), so she is Anna and Ms. Underwood is Dora. Dora does not work in Inventory (clue 6); she works in Accounts Receivable. By elimination, Brenda works in Inventory. In sum:

> Brenda Reese, Inventory
> Connie Stanley, Internal Auditing
> Anna Taylor, Accounts Payable
> Dora Underwood, Accounts Receivable

4. THRIFTY SHOPPERS

According to their purchases, the five women are: Emily, who bought rice at the Save More (clue 2); the Cost Less shopper, who bought flour and pickles for Ellen (clue 3); Louise, who bought chicken for Betty (clue 4); Ellen, who bought oranges and celery for Emily (clue 5); and the woman who bought potatoes and corn (clue 6). Since Louise does not shop at Save More (clue 2), Cost Less (clues 3, 4), Four Star, or Foodland (clue 1), she must shop at Tip Top. She then did not buy hamburger (clue 7); Emily must have bought that, and, by elimination, Louise bought bacon. The potatoes and corn were not bought for Louise (clue 6), so the rice and hamburger must have been. By elimination, the potatoes and corn were bought for Karen. Since Karen did not buy the specials for herself, she must be the Cost Less shopper, and Betty bought Karen's specials. Betty does not shop at Foodland (clue 4), so Ellen must, and Betty shops at Four Star. In summary:

> Betty—Four Star, potatoes and corn for Karen
> Ellen—Foodland, oranges and celery for Emily
> Emily—Save More, rice and hamburger for Louise
> Karen—Cost Less, flour and pickles for Ellen
> Louise—Tip Top, chicken and bacon for Betty

5. FOUR FENCES

Joe's isn't the westernmost house (clue 6). By clue 2, then, he can only live in the second house from the west end of the street, and Mr. Post lives in the one at the east end. Mr. Key cannot live between Mr. Post and Joe, because Joe did not build the lattice fence (clues 4, 6). So Mr. Key must be Joe and the lattice fence graces the last house on the west. Ed, who doesn't live next to Joe Key (clue 4), is Mr. Post. The house between Joe's and Ed's has a chain-link fence (clue 1). The picket fence isn't Ed's (clue 2) and must be Joe's, while Ed's fence is the horizontal board design. The chain-link fence is Marvin's (clue 3); he isn't Gates (clue 5), so he is Locke. By elimination, Tom is Gates and must have installed the lattice fence. In sum, from west to east:

> Tom Gates, lattice
> Joe Key, picket
> Marvin Locke, chain-link
> Ed Post, horizontal board

6. RURAL MISHAPS

Reston, who can only be the farmhand, was kicked by a mule (line 7). Thus, it was Farmer Brown who was bitten by a garter snake (lines 1–2); by line 5, that was the first of the five mishaps. Johnny is the son, and his was the third mishap (line 6). The beesting was the fourth mishap (line 9). By lines 11–12, Mrs. Brown wasn't stung, so she was the one butted by the cow—and since her mishap wasn't the last to occur, it must have been the second. By elimination, the farmhand's mishap was the last of the five, the bee's victim was Farmer Brown's daughter, and son Johnny was stung by the wasp. In sum, in the order in which the events occurred:

> 1. Farmer Brown, snakebite
> 2. Mrs. Brown, cow butt
> 3. Son (Johnny), wasp sting
> 4. Daughter, beesting
> 5. Farmhand (Reston), mule kick

7. THE GOLF COORDINATORS

Bill and Betty Ambrose's months are, respectively, either September and October or November and December (clue 2). There are no mixed events in December (clue 1), and by clue 3, Betty and White are cochairing an event; therefore, Bill's assignment is September and Betty's October, while White is the men's coordinator for October. Also by clue 3, Maureen and Clark are cochairing a mixed event, so they must be the two coordinators for November. By elimination, John Ashe is the men's coordinator for December. By clue 5, White's first name is Bob, and Clark's is Dick. By clue 6, Maureen's last name is Morrison, and Dora is the women's coordinator for September. The women's coordinator for December, by elimination, is Shirley. Shirley isn't Wallace (clue 4), so Dora is, and Shirley's last name is Flag. In sum:

Sept.: Bill Ambrose, Dora Wallace
Oct.: Bob White, Betty Ambrose
Nov.: Dick Clark, Maureen Morrison
Dec.: John Ashe, Shirley Flag

8. READ THE FINE PRINT!

According to clue 5, you have this order of the amount each paid: the NOW account, then Gloria, and then Butler. However the NOW account wasn't charged the most (clue 6), so Herbert, who paid $8, was. Butler didn't pay the least (also clue 6), so Mason, who paid $4, did. Thus, Herbert was charged the most, $8, the one with the NOW account was charged $7, Gloria $6, Butler $5, and Mason $4. Edward must have the NOW account, Herbert the super NOW account, and Butler the regular checking account (clue 2). Rhoda is not Butler (clue 1), so she is Mason, and Butler is Will. Gloria must be Ms. Cook, and since she does not have a passbook savings account (clue 3), Rhoda does, and Gloria has statement savings. Herbert is not Taylor (clue 4), so Edward is. By elimination, Herbert's last name is Carpenter. In sum, in order of the size of the charges:

Herbert Carpenter, super NOW, $8
Edward Taylor, NOW, $7
Gloria Cook, statement savings, $6
Will Butler, regular checking, $5
Rhoda Mason, passbook savings, $4

9. THE AQUARIUM VISIT

From clue 2, the Brown children are both boys and one is five years old. Sarah's last name must be Green, and Tommy, who is not her cousin (clue 5), must be her brother. The oldest is seven and is not Tommy Green (clue 4) or Sarah (clue 5), so the second Brown boy is seven. Matthew is the same age as another child (clue 1), so he cannot be the sole seven-year-old and must be the five-year-old Brown boy, and one of the Green children is also five. The seven-year-old, by elimination, is Daniel. The other Green child is six (clue 3). The child who liked the dolphins best isn't Tommy (clue 6). By clue 5, then, Sarah must be six, and Daniel liked the dolphin act best; Tommy is five. Neither Matthew (clue 1) nor Sarah (clue 3) liked the whales best, so Tommy did. Matthew also isn't the child who liked the seals best (clue 2), so Sarah did and Matthew, by elimination, preferred the walruses. In sum:

Daniel Brown, 7: dolphins
Matthew Brown, 5: walruses
Sarah Green, 6: seals
Tommy Green, 5: whales

10. PICKLES, PEARS, AND PEACHES, PLUS

There are eight different foods mentioned in the clues. Since each sister canned four different foods, and no food was canned by more than two of the women, the only possibility is that each of the eight foods was canned by *precisely* two. Andrea canned pears (clue 1), Debbie beans (clue 2) and Marcia strawberries (clue 3). Marcia also canned peaches, as did Eleanor (clue 7). Eleanor did not can pickles (clue 5); nor did Marcia (clue 8), so both Andrea and Debbie did. Also by clue 8, then, neither of the latter canned strawberries, so the second one who did was Eleanor. Neither Debbie (clue 2) nor Andrea (clue 6) canned peas, so Marcia and Eleanor both did. Again by clue 6, the two who canned corn were Marcia or Eleanor—but not both—and Debbie. By clue 4, Debbie did not can carrots, and the two who did must have been Andrea and either Marcia or Eleanor; Marcia didn't (clue 9), so Eleanor did, and Marcia canned corn. By elimination, Andrea's fourth food was beans and Debbie's was pears. In sum:

141

Andrea: beans, carrots, pears, pickles
Debbie: beans, corn, pears, pickles
Eleanor: carrots, peaches, peas, strawberries
Marcia: corn, peaches, peas, strawberries

11. A PUZZLE PUZZLER

We are told (line 2) that the book contained three logic problems, which were labeled I, II, and III. The second verse tells us that each of the seven members of the family solved one or more of the problems, but that no two family members solved precisely the same problems. This means that: one person in the family solved all three problems; three family members each solved two problems (I and II, I and III, or II and III); and three family members solved one problem, each a different one. Problem III was not solved by Cal, Betsy, or Mr. Ames (lines 13–14); so one of them solved I only, one solved II only, and one solved I and II. By lines 17–18, Cal solved a problem that Betsy did not do and vice versa, so each must have solved one problem, and Mr. Ames solved both I and II. Lines 21–22 tell us that Cal solved problem I, so Betsy did problem II. Jimmy did only one problem (line 23), so he must have done III. Brad solved a puzzle that Sue did not solve and vice versa (lines 19–20), so it was neither Brad nor Sue who did all three of the problems; by elimination, it was Mrs. Ames. Brad and Sue each solved two puzzles, and Brad did not solve I (lines 15–16); so Brad solved II and III, while Sue solved I and III. In sum:

> Mrs. Ames: all three
> Mr. Ames: I and II
> Betsy: II
> Brad: II and III
> Cal: I
> Jimmy: III
> Sue: I and III

12. 002'S RENDEZVOUS

By clue 3, two ladies came from opposite directions—i.e., either east and west or north and south—at 9:00 P.M. and 10:00 P.M., and the other two at 11:00 P.M. and midnight; one of these pairs was Tess and the lady in blue. By clue 4, the lady in blue arrived an hour before Enid; her rendezvous can only have been at 10:00 P.M., Tess's at 9:00 P.M., and Enid's at 11:00 P.M. The lady in blue was Maria, and Enid wore green (clue 1). The lady in red came at 9:00 P.M. (clue 2). By elimination, Carmen was the midnight lady, and she wore yellow. By clue 2, she and Enid used the north and south paths, so Tess and Maria arrived from east and west. By clue 4, Maria didn't use the western path; she used the eastern and Tess the western. By the same clue, Enid used the northern path, so Carmen used the path from the south. In sum, in order of arrival from 9:00 P.M. to midnight:

> Tess: red, west
> Maria: blue, east
> Enid: green, north
> Carmen: yellow, south

13. UNITED STATES STAMPS

Stamps honoring nine people are mentioned. Since three of them cost 15¢ each (clue 5) and we are told that at least two have been on each denomination stamp (clue 5), the other six people must be on no more than three denominations, so there are four or fewer denominations. The Grandma Moses stamp cost 2¢ less than the Willa Cather stamp, which cost 5¢ less than the Carl Sandburg stamp (clue 1). By clue 3, the Harriet Tubman stamp cost the same as the Carl Sandburg stamp, and the John Steinbeck stamp cost 2¢ more than that. We now have four denominations, so there are no others. By clue 2, the Walt Disney stamp can only have cost the same as the Grandma Moses stamp, the John Sloan stamp the same as the Willa Cather stamp, and the Frances Perkins stamp the same as the John Steinbeck stamp. The Dolley Madison stamp also cost the same as the John Steinbeck stamp (clue 4), and that figure was 15¢ (clue 5). The Sandburg and Tubman stamps then cost 13¢, the Cather and Sloan stamps 8¢, and the Grandma Moses and Disney stamps 6¢. In sum:

> 6¢: Walt Disney, Grandma Moses
> 8¢: Willa Cather, John Sloan
> 13¢: Carl Sandburg, Harriet Tubman
> 15¢: Dolley Madison, Frances Perkins, John Steinbeck

14. THE AUBREY SISTERS

By clue 5, the five sisters are Angela, the one who collects rocks, the one who plays the piano, the one studying French, and the one who plays the guitar. Andrea, who plays the violin and does not speak French (clue 4), must be the rock collector. The flute player who is studying German (clue 2) must be Angela. The pianist collects butterflies (clue 6). The one who is learning Russian and collects old buttons (clue 1) must be the guitarist. Anne, who collects coins (clue 3), is then the one who is studying French. Alice, who studies Italian (clue 7) must be the pianist. By elimination, the guitarist is Amy, Anne plays the harp, Andrea studies Spanish, and Angela collects stamps. In sum:

> Alice: piano, Italian, butterflies
> Amy: guitar, Russian, buttons
> Andrea: violin, Spanish, rocks
> Angela: flute, German, stamps
> Anne: harp, French, coins

15. VIDEO ARCADE CONTEST

The five winners were Scott, the Booth boy, the girl who played Starflight against Oscar, the Cole child, and Kate (clue 1). By clue 2, Ginger, who defeated the Jarvis girl, can only be the Cole child, so Doug, who won against the Hale boy, must be the Booth boy. The Field boy, who won (clue 4), must be Scott. Neither Kate nor Ginger Cole played Submarines (clue 1). By clue 5, then, Cathy played against Scott Field and—since there are five boys and five girls—Amy, who played Journey, is the Jarvis girl; the girl who played Starflight and defeated Oscar, by elimination, is Jessica. Doug didn't win at Grabbin' Gators (clue 2), so Kate did, and Doug must have played Air Attack. Doug played against Keith (clue 5). The boy who lost to Kate, by elimination, is Nathan. By clue 3, the Ellis boy isn't Nathan and must be Oscar, while Jessica's last name is Grant. By clue 4, Kate's last name is Aster, and the Keats child must be Cathy; Nathan's last name, by elimination, is Day. In sum:

GAME	WINNER	LOSER
Air Attack	Doug Booth	Keith Hale
Grabbin' Gators	Kate Aster	Nathan Day
Journey	Ginger Cole	Amy Jarvis
Starflight	Jessica Grant	Oscar Ellis
Submarines	Scott Field	Cathy Keats

16. THE WEBSTER CONNECTION

The first one to give definitions was the Nagle boy, one of whose words was *sapsago* (clue 5). By clue 1, Amy, who defined *nekton,* was second; the Nagle boy's second word was *clinquant;* Charles Palmer was third; and Don was fourth. Since three of the six are boys, the Nagle boy must be Bob. The Mason child, who defined *pecksniffian,* was sixth (clue 3). Bella Long can only have been fifth; she defined *doppelgänger* and *locofoco* (clue 2). The Roper child, who defined *jugulum* and *thermotaxis* (clue 4), must be Don. Charles Palmer defined *hippogriff* and *whiffet* (clue 6). By elimination, Amy's last name is Kern and the Mason girl's first name is Cora. Amy's second word was *acrophobia* and Cora's was *gallipot* (clue 7) In sum, in order:

Bob Nagle:
    clinquant—adj., [archaic], glittering as with gold or silver
    sapsago—n., hard, greenish cheese
Amy Kern:
    acrophobia—n., fear of heights
    nekton—n., all the larger aquatic, free-swimming animals
Charles Palmer:
    hippogriff—n., mythical monster with head and wings of a griffin and hindquarters of a horse
    whiffet—n., an insignificant, esp. young, person
Don Roper:
    jugulum—n., the lower throat
    thermotaxis—n., normal regulation of body temperature
Bella Long:
    doppelgänger—n., ghostly double of a living person
    locofoco—n., orig., a match ignited by friction; later, (L-) a Democrat, circa 1835, from the use of such matches in Tammany Hall
Cora Mason:
    gallipot—n., a small usually ceramic vessel with a small mouth
    pecksniffian—adj., (often cap) [after Dickens's character Seth Pecksniff] hypocritical

17. HELPING THE ELDERLY

By clue 1, three boys did painting: a 14-year-old, whose gift was fudge; Bobby; and the Smith boy. The two others are one who grocery-shopped, who isn't Pete, and Carl (clue 3); Carl must have mowed the lawn. Pete isn't the Smith boy (clue 5), so he can only be the boy who got the fudge, and the Smith boy is also 14 (clue 5). By clue 3, the boy who grocery-shopped is 15, and Carl is 16. By clue 9, then, Bobby (who did painting, remember) can only be the 15-year-old Norton boy. We now know two of the boys are 14, two 15, and one 16. By clue 8, the Smith boy must be Andy, and Carl got an apple pie. The one who grocery-shopped, by elimination, is Kenny. He didn't get the oatmeal cookies or the scarf (clue 6), so his gift was the chocolate chip cookies. Andy didn't get the scarf (clue 7), so Bobby did, and Andy got the oatmeal cookies. The latter didn't paint the garage (clue 4) or the shutters (clue 7); he painted the fence. Since Carl got the pie, his last name isn't Bailey or Illes (clue 2) and can only be Young. Pete's last name isn't Bailey (clue 3), so Kenny's is, and Pete's is Illes. Pete didn't paint the garage (clue 2), so Bobby did, and Pete painted the shutters. In sum:

        Kenny Bailey, 15: grocery-shopped, chocolate chip cookies
        Pete Illes, 14: painted shutters, fudge
        Bobby Norton, 15: painted garage, scarf
        Andy Smith, 14: painted fence, oatmeal cookies
        Carl Young, 16: mowed lawn, apple pie

18. REAL ESTATE

The final selling prices were $92,000 (given), $76,000 (clue 7), $63,000 (clue 1), $50,000 (clue 8), and $46,000 (clue 4). Only one price is twice another, so the Adamses paid $92,000, and the Flynns received $46,000 in the transaction handled by Debbie (clue 3). The only prices equally separated are $50,000, $63,000, and $76,000, so, by clue 5, the Halls paid $50,000 and the Spears sold their home for $76,000; the latter was the duplex purchased by the Taylors (clue 7). The Halls bought the beach cottage, and Jack was the agent (clue 8). The Meyers didn't pay $63,000 (clue 5), so they must have purchased the Flynns' home, and the Simons paid the $63,000. Neither the Simons nor the Meyers bought the condominium (clue 4), so the Adamses did. Jane didn't handle the sale to the Taylors or the $63,000 sale to the Simons (clue 1), so she sold the condominium. The agent handling the duplex wasn't Alice (clue 7) and must have been Robert, while Alice handled the sale to the Simons. Neither Alice (clue 6) nor Jack (clue 8) worked for the Uptons, so Jane did. The Halls didn't buy from the Bakers (clue 2); they bought from the Reids, and the Bakers sold to the Simons. The Flynns' home was the ranch style, the Bakers' was the trilevel (clue 3). In sum:

> Jane sold the Uptons' condominium to the Adamses for $92,000.
> Robert sold the Spears' duplex to the Taylors for $76,000.
> Alice sold the Bakers' trilevel to the Simons for $63,000.
> Jack sold the Reids' beach cottage to the Halls for $50,000.
> Debbie sold the Flynns' ranch style to the Meyers for $46,000.

19. HOLIDAZE

The twins born on March 17th are both boys, those born on July 4th both girls (clue 2). Those born on October 31st weighed a total of 8 pounds (clue 6). The twins born on December 25th are Becky and her brother, who together weighed 7½ pounds (clue 4). Carol and Jason, who together weighed 7 pounds and were not born on February 14th (clue 1), must have been born on January 1st. The combined birth weight of John Allen and his sister was then 8 pounds (clue 5), so they were born October 31st. We have accounted for the sexes of five sets of twins: one pair of boys, one pair of girls, and three brother-sister pairs; since there are only five boys' names mentioned, the sixth pair of twins—the set born February 14th—are both girls. From clue 8, there is only one possibility: Debra Taylor is one of the girls born February 14th; Kathy and her sister were born July 4th; and Brad Wilkes is Becky's brother. By elimination, David and Kevin are the boys born March 17th. John Allen's sister is neither Susan nor Patty (clue 5); she is Mary. Kathy's sister is not Susan (clue 8), so she is Patty, and Susan is Debra Taylor's sister. Kathy and Patty are the Stuart girls (clue 7). Since Carol and Jason together weighed 7 pounds, the Hollis twins, whose combined weight was 9½ pounds (clue 3), must be David and Kevin; the Stuart twins' combined weight was then 8½ pounds (clue 7). By elimination, the Taylor girls' combined weight was 10 pounds and Carol's and Jason's last name is Barnes. In sum:

> 1/1 Carol and Jason Barnes, 7 lbs.
> 2/14 Debra and Susan Taylor, 10 lbs.
> 3/17 David and Kevin Hollis, 9½ lbs.
> 7/4 Kathy and Patty Stuart, 8½ lbs.
> 10/31 John and Mary Allen, 8 lbs.
> 12/25 Becky and Brad Wilkes, 7½ lbs.

20. AT THE COUNTY FAIR

By clue 1, the boy who spent $11 had $9 left, so he started with $20. He is not Dan (clue 2), Bud, Ken, or Tim (clue 3), so he is Joe. Since all amounts are in whole dollars, Bud, Ken, and Tim each must have started with an even number of dollars in order for each to spend the same amount as he had left (clue 3), so the boy who started with an odd amount (clue 4) must be Dan. He spent twice as much as he had left (clue 2), so his original amount had to be divisible by three and can only have been $15; thus, he spent $10 and had $5 left. Tim also had $5 left (clue 5), and since he spent half his money, he started with $10. Bud spent $1 more than Tim (clue 6), so he started with $12 and spent $6. Ken, as mentioned earlier, started with an even number of dollars so by clue 7, he started with $8 more than an even number. He must have started with $8 more than the $6 Bud had left—i.e., $14—and spent $7. In sum:

> Joe had $20, spent $11
> Dan had $15, spent $10
> Ken had $14, spent $7
> Bud had $12, spent $6
> Tim had $10, spent $5

21. BRIDAL ATTENDANTS

The least number of attendants a bride had was one (intro). That bride was not Mrs. Oliver (clue 2), Mrs. Kelly, Mrs. Neuman (clue 4), or Mrs. Likens (clue 6), so she was Mrs. Morris. By clue 1, then, Gary's bride had three attendants and Carla five. Mrs. Morris is not Ellen (clue 4), Betty, or Doris (clue 5), so she is Anna. Her husband is not Isaac (clue 2), Jack, or Frank (clue 3), so he is Howard. By clue 4, then, Mrs. Kelly had two attendants, Ellen is Gary's wife, and Mrs. Neuman had six attendants. By clue 2, the only possibility is that Doris is Mrs. Kelly, Mrs. Oliver is Ellen, and Isaac is Carla's husband. By elimination, Mrs. Neuman is Betty, and Carla's and Isaac's last name is Likens. Betty's husband is Jack, and Doris's is Frank (clue 3). In sum:

> Betty and Jack Neuman, 6
> Carla and Isaac Likens, 5
> Ellen and Gary Oliver, 3
> Doris and Frank Kelly, 2
> Anna and Howard Morris, 1

22. ONCE AROUND WILDE LAKE

By clue 3, Jill, Margot, and the jogger are three different people. By clue 4, the fourth person is Meg, she and the jogger proceeded clockwise around the lake, and Chang is either Jill or Margot. The jogger, by elimination, is Jerry. By clue 1, two of the four, who must have been Margot and Jill, walked counterclockwise; Jill pushed the baby carriage; and Margot's last name is Pratt, so Jill is Chang. By clue 2, Bosen must be Meg, and she was the dog walker; by elimination, Margot was the bird watcher, and Jerry's last name is Sachs. Clue 2 also tells us that Meg passed the dock before Jerry did, Jerry then passed the dock and overtook Meg, and then Margot appeared coming from the opposite direction. By clue 3, Jill was behind Margot and did not overtake her (clue 1), so Margot reached the dock third, Jill last. In sum, in order of reaching the dock:

> Meg Bosen, dog walker
> Jerry Sachs, jogger
> Margot Pratt, bird watcher
> Jill Chang, carriage pusher

23. FLOWERS FOR THE DANCE

The three girls are Ann, the Marsh girl, and the one who wore the white gardenias (clue 4). Bea didn't wear white flowers since her third dance was with the boy with the white boutonniere (clue 2), so she is the Marsh girl, and Donna wore the white gardenias. Donna's date with his white boutonniere, then, must have had the second dance with Ann, so the Harris girl, whose second partner wore a red boutonniere (clue 3), is Donna, and Ann's last name is Cox. Bea Marsh's second partner, by elimination, wore a purple flower, so she was the one who wore a corsage of red roses, while Ann wore the purple orchid. The Rowe boy, Bea's partner for the second dance (clue 2), was then Ann's escort. From clue 1, Ann's second partner was Rob, and since we have established that her second partner wore white, he must be Donna's date and her third, the Evans boy, must have been Bea's escort. Donna Harris's third partner, George (clue 3), was then Ann's escort. By elimination, the Evans boy's first name is John and Rob's surname is Sloan. In sum, with each girl's partners, in order, for the first three dances:

> Ann Cox, purple orchid: George Rowe, Rob, John
> Bea Marsh, red roses: John Evans, George, Rob
> Donna Harris, white gardenias: Rob Sloan, John, George

24. THE RHYMESTERS

The first three to finish their rhymes were Joe, the pupil who used the word *tame*, and the girl who used *home* (clue 1). The last of the six was Bess Longfellow, who used *gnome* (clue 2). A fifth child is Ellen, who used *game* and *loam* (clue 3). Since three boys and three girls are mentioned, Amy must be the girl who finished third and used *home* (clue 1), and a sixth child, who, like Ellen, finished fourth or fifth, is a boy. The Kilmer child, who used *comb*, isn't Amy (she used *home*), Ellen (clue 3), Dick (clue 4), or Joe (clue 1), so Roger is the Kilmer child, and must have finished second (clue 4) and used *tame* (clue 1), while Dick is the sixth child referred to above and used *aim* (clue 4). Amy, who used *home*, isn't the Shelley child (clue 5), nor is the Shelley child, who used *dame*, Dick (*aim*) or Ellen (clue 3); Joe is Shelley. Since Joe Shelley didn't use *foam*, Dick did and Joe, by elimination, used *dome*. Amy didn't use *blame* (clue 6) so Bess did, while Amy used *name*. The Whittier child must be Amy (clue 7). Dick is not Keats (clue 4) so Ellen is, and she finished fourth (clue 7). Dick is then Burns, and he finished fifth. In sum, in the order of finish:

> Joe Shelley: dame, dome
> Roger Kilmer: tame, comb
> Amy Whittier: name, home
> Ellen Keats: game, loam
> Dick Burns: aim, foam
> Bess Longfellow: blame, gnome

25. MRS. FINNEGAN'S BOARDERS

Bob and Chuck both have ham (clue 2), and Bob has coffee (clue 5). Ned has eggs (clue 4). By clue 1, Al has either ham or bacon, and a fifth boarder breakfasts on pancakes and bacon. The latter isn't Peter (clue 3), so he is Will, and Peter is the sixth boarder. By clue 6, there are two who have sausage and tea, and they can only be Ned and Peter; since no two have exactly the same breakfast, Peter must have pancakes. Also by clue 6, since Bob drinks coffee, he has pancakes. Since Mrs. Finnegan will not cook bacon for Will alone, Al has bacon. Both Chuck and Al have eggs (clue 7). Again by clue 6, then, Will has coffee, and Chuck and Al have milk. In sum:

> Al: eggs, bacon, milk
> Bob: pancakes, ham, coffee
> Chuck: eggs, ham, milk
> Ned: eggs, sausage, tea
> Peter: pancakes, sausage, tea
> Will: pancakes, bacon, coffee

26. IT'S A TRIP

By clue 1, John and his wife Bev visited Hawaii and the Bahamas; a second couple, the Becks, also visited Hawaii; and a third couple, Wilma Eastman and her husband, also visited the Bahamas. By clue 3, a fourth couple, Jim and his wife, who traveled aboard the *Illinois*, visited Tahiti and Bermuda; the Eastmans' second port of call was Tahiti; and Burt and Mary, who—since they are not the Becks—are the fifth couple and visited Bermuda. By clue 2, June and her husband, who went to St. Thomas, must be the Becks, and the couple who traveled on the *California* and also visited St. Thomas can only be Burt and Mary; since Dave isn't June's husband, he is Wilma's. By clue 4, the Taylors, who traveled aboard the *Montana*, can only be John and Bev, and the *Washington*, which also went to Hawaii, must be the ship on which the Becks traveled. Since Mary and Burt aren't the Simpsons (clue 3), they are the Wileys, and Jim and his wife are the Simpsons. By elimination, June's husband is Mike, Jim's wife is Goldie, and the Eastmans traveled aboard the *New York*. In sum:

Mike and June Beck: *Washington*, Hawaii and St. Thomas
Dave and Wilma Eastman: *New York*, Bahamas and Tahiti
Jim and Goldie Simpson: *Illinois*, Bermuda and Tahiti
John and Bev Taylor: *Montana*, Bahamas and Hawaii
Burt and Mary Wiley: *California*, Bermuda and St. Thomas

27. REDECORATING

By clue 6, Bev lives at 105 and the woman who bought the carpeting at 107. By clue 4, then, the latter is Dee, and the one who bought the mirror tiles lives at 103. The woman at 103 is Flo, Bev bought the bamboo shades, and Dee bought the carpeting for her bathroom (clue 1). By clue 2, Kit's address can't be 104, since only 103 is lower, so it is 106. Also by clue 2, since Flo, at 103, is not redoing her study, the study is in 104 and Bev is Mrs. Tuley. By elimination, Jan is redecorating her study. By clue 5, Kit's last name is Swift and Dee's is Lynch, and Flo is redecorating her kitchen. Jan's last name is Mitchell, and Kit Swift bought a chandelier (clue 1) for her living room (clue 3). By elimination, Jan Mitchell bought the paneling, Flo's last name is Riley, and Bev Tuley is redecorating a bedroom. In sum:

> 103, Flo Riley: mirror tiles, kitchen
> 104, Jan Mitchell: paneling, study
> 105, Bev Tuley: bamboo shades, bedroom
> 106, Kit Swift: chandelier, living room
> 107, Dee Lynch: carpeting, bathroom

28. GENTLEMEN CHEFS

Clue 1 lists all six chefs. Three—Jim, Mr. Parsons, and Carol's husband—live on the north side of the fairway; the other three—Jack, Mr. Baker, and the one whose specialty is Caesar salad—live on the south side. By clue 3, Mr. Linden, whose specialty is nut bread, lives on the south side; he must be Jack. By clue 5, Matt Jones's specialty is meat loaf, so he can only be Carol's husband. Jane lives next door to the Joneses (clue 4)—i.e., on the north side of the fairway; since she isn't Jim's wife (clue 3) she is Mrs. Parsons. Doris and George, whose specialty is Brunswick stew (clue 2), must be the Bakers. Mr. Parsons isn't Max (clue 1), so he is Joe, and Max is the Caesar-salad maker. Sourdough bread isn't Joe Parsons's specialty (clue 4); it must be Jim's, and Joe's is clam chowder. Since George lives on the south side of the fairway, Mr. Clark lives on the north side (clue 6) and must be Jim. Max's last name, by elimination, is Roper. By clue 7, Betty and Penny live on the same side of the fairway, so that is the south side—and since Betty isn't Max Roper's wife, Penny is, and Betty is Mrs. Linden. Mrs. Clark, by elimination, is Myra. In sum:

> Doris and George Baker, Brunswick stew
> Myra and Jim Clark, sourdough bread
> Carol and Matt Jones, meat loaf
> Betty and Jack Linden, nut bread
> Jane and Joe Parsons, clam chowder
> Penny and Max Roper, Caesar salad

29. TRACTS AND TREES

By clue 2, the down payments of six of the buyers are $1,500, $2,000, $2,500, $3,000, $3,500, and $4,000, and the down payment by the seventh buyer duplicates one of these amounts. By clue 5, Parks, who was the only one to make a down payment of $2,000, chose an elm tree. By clue 3, then, Brady, who chose a cypress, must have made a down payment of $3,500, while Newton, who chose a lemon tree and a cypress, made a down payment of $1,500. Again since only Parks's down payment was $2,000, by clue 4 Hammer's must have been $1,500 and that of the buyer

148

who chose the lemon tree and the elm $3,000; by the same clue, one of Hammer's selections is a plum tree. The down payments not mentioned thus far are $2,500 and $4,000. By clue 6, Sloan, who chose an elm tree, must have made the $4,000 down payment; the $3,000 must have been paid by Allerton; and the one who chose the lemon tree and the pine—by elimination, Barnes—paid the $2,500. Each buyer chose one fruit tree (clue 1), two of them cherry trees (clue 7); the latter do not include Parks (clue 5), so they are Brady and Sloan. By clue 7, then, Parks's second tree is a lime and Hammer's is an oak. In sum:

> Sloan: $4,000, cherry and elm
> Brady: $3,500, cherry and cypress
> Allerton: $3,000, lemon and elm
> Barnes: $2,500, lemon and pine
> Parks: $2,000, lime and elm
> Hammer: $1,500, plum and oak
> Newton: $1,500, lemon and cypress

30. REQUEST TIME

The fifth song requested was not "Smoke Gets in the Wind" (clue 1), "Tears on the Clock" (clue 3), "Rock Around Little Susie" (clue 5), or "Blowin' in Your Eyes" (clue 6), so it was "Wake Up My Pillow." These three songs were requested before at least two others: "Smoke Gets in the Wind" (clue 1), "Rock Around Little Susie" (clue 5) and "Blowin' in Your Eyes" (clue 6); so "Tears on the Clock" was the fourth request. Therefore, by clue 3, Trudy was the third woman to make a request and Mark was the fifth band member to receive a request. Now, the only possibility by clue 1 is that "Smoke Gets in the Wind" was the first song requested, Jane was the second woman to make a request, and Eric received Trudy's request. By clue 5, Andy received a request after someone requested "Rock Around Little Susie," so he was the fourth band member to receive a request. Chris, then, received the second request and Nola was the first woman to request a song (clue 2). By elimination, Nola made her request of Barry. By clue 4, then, Sue made the fourth request, and Mark is the piano player. By elimination, it was Barb who spoke to Mark. Once again, by clue 5, Andy, who we know took the fourth request, and the guitar player both received requests after the drummer received a request for "Rock Around Little Susie." Therefore, the only possibility is that Chris received the request for "Rock Around Little Susie," and is the drummer, and that the guitar player is Eric. By this same clue, we know Andy plays an instrument, so he is the saxophonist, and Barry is the lead singer; "Blowin' in Your Eyes," by elimination, was the third song requested. In sum, in the order requested:

> "Smoke Gets in the Wind," Nola, lead singer Barry
> "Rock Around Little Susie," Jane, drummer Chris
> "Blowin' in Your Eyes," Trudy, guitarist Eric
> "Tears on the Clock," Sue, saxophonist Andy
> "Wake Up My Pillow," Barb, pianist Mark

31. BEINGS FROM ANOTHER GALAXY

The yonix in the purple spaceship bought fifty fuel pellets (clue 3). By clue 6, the one in the orange spaceship bought forty, the one from the planet Diatis twenty, and Droc ten. The one from the planet Zucon, then, bought thirty (clue 1). Droc can only be the one in the blue spaceship from the planet Tyrus (clue 5). By clue 2, the yonix from Pluriz must be the one in the purple spaceship, while Uris is from Diatis; since the latter's ship isn't the green one, the Zucon ship is. By elimination, the Diatis ship is silver, and the orange ship is from Quazin. Exis must be from Zucon (clue 4). Boiz is not from Pluriz (clue 2), so Ando is, and Boiz is from Quazin. In sum:

> Ando from Pluriz: purple, 50
> Boiz from Quazin: orange, 40
> Exis from Zucon: green, 30
> Uris from Diatis: silver, 20
> Droc from Tyrus: blue, 10

By clue 5, the second prize entry is the middle one of five. By clue 2, there are at least three entries to the left of June's, and Ms. Block's, to the immediate left of June's, is not the second-prize entry in the center; June's entry is therefore at the extreme right, and the pie is second from the left—and, since none of these has won the grand prize, that prize has gone to the entry at the extreme left. By clue 5, then, Ms. Wilson's entry won the grand prize, June's won the honorable mention, and the layer cake is Ms. Block's entry. May is the second-prize winner, and Ms. Ives baked the pie (clue 3). By clue 1, Marion can only be Ms. Wilson, and Myra is Ms. Block; by elimination, Irene is Ms. Ives. Irene Ives's pie has won first prize, May's last name is Martin, and June made the tarts (clue 4); by elimination, Myra Block's cake has won third prize, and June's last name is Sims. May Martin didn't make the pickles (clue 3), so she made the preserves, and Marion Wilson made the pickles. In sum from left to right:

> Marion Wilson's pickles, grand prize
> Irene Ives's pie, first prize
> May Martin's preserves, second prize
> Myra Block's cake, third prize
> June Sims's tarts, honorable mention

33.   THE PRINCESSES AND THE DRAGONS

Princess Genevieve was rescued by the Prince of Nottingham (clue 1). Princess Catherine was captured by Trollkarl (clue 4). Princess Genevieve was not captured by Brujo (clue 1) or Shrayik (clue 2), so the dragon that captured her was Gespent, and she was Princess of Berkshire (clue 8). Winifred was Princess of Lancashire (clue 5). Since Prince Lionel rescued Princess Regina (clue 6), and the Princess of Cheshire was rescued by Prince Geoffrey (clue 3), the Princess of Cheshire can only have been Catherine. By elimination, Regina was Princess of Shropshire. Prince Erwin of Huntingham (clue 7) can only have rescued Princess Winifred. By elimination, the Prince of Nottingham was Nathan. The Prince of Durham, who fought Shrayik (clue 2), must have been Lionel. By elimination, Princess Winifred was captured by Brujo and Geoffrey was Prince of Chippenham. In sum:

> Genevieve of Berkshire: Gespent; Nathan of Nottingham
> Catherine of Cheshire: Trollkarl; Geoffrey of Chippenham
> Winifred of Lancashire: Brujo; Erwin of Huntingham
> Regina of Shropshire: Shrayik; Lionel of Durham

34.   VACATION VISITS

Consecutive visits were made to Annie and her husband and Bill and his wife; neither was to Madison (clue 1). By clue 6, the visit to Madison wasn't the first and was immediately followed by the visit to Bruce and his wife, which was not the last (clue 3). The only possibility is that the second visit was to Madison, the third to Annie and her husband Bruce, and the fourth to Bill and his wife. The first was to the Wangs (clue 6). Mrs. Wang isn't Sally or Jane (clue 2), so she is Alice. By clue 7, Jane lives in Madison, and the Bakers were one of the last two couples visited; Bill's wife, by elimination, is Sally. Sally and Bill aren't the Bakers (clue 4), so Annie and Bruce are. The Wangs live in Chatham (also clue 4). Sally and Bill don't live in Concord (clue 2), so they live in Columbia and the Bakers in Concord. Sally and Bill aren't the Smiths, nor is Mr. Smith Bob (clue 5); Sally and Bill are the Golds, Jane is Mrs. Smith, and Bob must be Mr. Wang. Jane's husband, by elimination, is Dave. In sum, in order of visits:

> Alice and Bob Wang, Chatham
> Jane and Dave Smith, Madison
> Annie and Bruce Baker, Concord
> Sally and Bill Gold, Columbia

35. RECOGNITION DINNER

The two who had been with Gibbon the longest were retiring (clue 5). Two others, Shirley and Anderson, were being promoted (clue 3). By clue 2, Miller is a man but is not Frank, so—since only two men are mentioned—he is Brian; at least two of the five had been with the company longer, so he is not one of the retirees. He must be the one described in clue 1; Brian Miller was with Gibbon 10 years and has taken a job with a different company. Crosby has been with Gibbon for 20 years. Frank for 25 (clue 2). Clue 4, like clue 2, mentions three people—Wolfe, Doreen, and an unnamed person who had been with Gibbon 5 years fewer than Doreen. Since there are a total of five, at least one of those mentioned in clue 2 must also be mentioned in clue 4. Frank can't be Wolfe, since Frank was there an odd number of years (clue 2) and Wolfe an even number of years (clue 4). If Frank were the one who'd been with Gibbon 5 years fewer than Doreen, then Wolfe would have been there 60 years, contradicting clue 5. Crosby can't be the one who was there 5 years fewer than Doreen, since Frank and Doreen would have then been there the same number of years. If Doreen were Crosby, then Wolfe, 40 years, and Frank, 25 years, would be the two retirees; Doreen Crosby, 20 years, would be one of the two who received promotions. But this contradicts clue 3. Thus, Brian Miller must be the one with 5 years' fewer tenure than Doreen, and the latter had been at Gibbon 15 years, while Wolfe had been there 30; the retirees are Wolfe and Frank. By clue 3, Crosby is Shirley, and Doreen is Anderson. By elimination, Wolfe's first name is Carol, and Frank's surname is Norris. In sum:

> 30 yrs.: Carol Wolfe, retiring
> 25 yrs.: Frank Norris, retiring
> 20 yrs.: Shirley Crosby, promoted
> 15 yrs.: Doreen Anderson, promoted
> 10 yrs.: Brian Miller, new job

36. SWEETS AND STUDIES

Since none of the girls ate fewer than two or more than eight cookies, the only possible conclusion from clue 6 is that Sharon ate four, the girl to her right two, and the girl who ate oatmeal cookies eight. Since all ate different numbers of cookies, Sharon who ate twice as many cookies as the girl to the right (clue 6) isn't the girl who ate the peanut butter cookies and ate twice as many cookies as the girl to her *left* (clue 1). Therefore, the girl who ate the peanut butter cookies must have eaten six, and the girl to her left ate three cookies. Only one of the possible numbers is three times another, so by clue 3, Pam ate the six peanut butter cookies, and the girl directly across from her ate two cookies; that girl was Mary (clue 4), and Sharon sat at Mary's left. Mary ate marshmallow cookies, and Jill sat to Mary's right (clue 2). Dolly, who ate five cookies (clue 5), must have sat between Pam and Sharon. The one who ate the eight oatmeal cookies must have been Jill. Sharon's cookies were butterscotch (clue 4). The girl who sat between Pam and Jill, by elimination, was Rita; her cookies must have been the lemon bars (clue 5), and Dolly's were chocolate chip. In sum, clockwise around the table:

> Pam, 6 peanut butter
> Rita, 3 lemon bars
> Jill, 8 oatmeal
> Mary, 2 marshmallow
> Sharon, 4 butterscotch
> Dolly, 5 chocolate chip

37. SUMMER JOB SCHEDULE

Since we know the siblings worked different numbers of hours, each a multiple of ten, and the weekly total was 100 hours, the four must have worked 10, 20, 30, and 40 hours. By clue 3, one girl worked 20 hours, the cashier worked 30, Jack worked either 10 or 40, and the sibling who had Mondays and Wednesdays off also either worked 10 or 40. By clue 1, the latter worked 10 hours and Jack worked 40. Clue 2 tells us that the baby-sitter was a boy and didn't work 40 hours, so he is Tom and must be the one who worked 10 hours. Also by clue 2, the cashier was a girl, and was off Tuesdays and Thursdays; the girl stable hand must have worked 20 hours a week. Jack, by elimination, was the lifeguard. Holly was the stable hand, who worked Sundays (clue 4), while Kate was the cashier. Since Wednesday was the only day two siblings were off, one was off each other day, so Jack must have had Sundays off. We know Tom was off Mondays, so Jack's second day off was Saturday (clue 1). Holly then had Fridays off and was the second sibling to have Wednesdays off. In sum:

> Holly: stable hand, 20 hrs., Wed. and Fri. off
> Jack: lifeguard, 40 hrs., Sat. and Sun. off
> Kate: cashier, 30 hrs., Tues. and Thurs. off
> Tom: baby-sitter, 10 hrs., Mon. and Wed. off

38. VICTORY AT SUNRISE VALLEY HIGH

By clue 2, the Benson boy scored ten fewer points than Danny and twice as many as Rob—i.e., an even number. A fourth boy, Luke, scored fifteen points (clue 3), and the high scorer was Vince (clue 5). The Benson boy, by elimination, is Lenny. The Nelson boy scored twenty points and is not Vince (clue 1), so he is either Danny or Rob. If he were Rob, then Lenny Benson would have scored forty points and Danny fifty—impossible, since the team's total score was seventy-five points. The Nelson boy is thus Danny, Lenny Benson scored ten points and Rob five. Vince scored the remaining twenty-five points. Vince is a guard (clue 1). Luke plays center (clue 5). Lenny is the second guard (clue 4); the two forwards, by elimination, are Danny and Rob. By clue 6, Rob's last name is Stevens and Luke's is Carson; Vince's, by elimination, is Hudson. In sum:

> Vince Hudson, guard, 25
> Danny Nelson, forward, 20
> Luke Carson, center, 15
> Lenny Benson, guard, 10
> Rob Stevens, forward, 5

39. THE THREE-LEGGED RACE

By clue 6, Ian and Sara were partners. Neither Chad (clue 2), Gary (clue 5), nor David (clue 7) was part of the fourth- or fifth-place pair, so Ian and Jack and their partners were fourth and fifth, in one order or the other. By clue 2, if Chad and his partner had been third, then Mandy and Jack would have been fourth and Ian and Sara fifth for the yellow team—contradicting clue 6. By clue 5, if Gary and his partner had been third, Karen and Jack would have been fourth—contradicting clue 1. Thus, David and his partner were third; Ian and Sara from the green team were fourth and Jack and Jill fifth (clue 7). By clue 3, the red team pair finished immediately ahead of the blue team pair, who weren't David and his partner; therefore, the red team pair placed first and the blue team pair second. Jack and Jill represented the yellow team and David and his partner, the orange team (clue 4). Gary and his teammate were on the blue team (clue 8), so David's partner was Karen (clue 5). By clue 2, Chad and his partner, by elimination, Lisa, finished first, and Mandy was Gary's partner. In sum, in order of finish:

> 1. Chad and Lisa, red
> 2. Gary and Mandy, blue
> 3. David and Karen, orange
> 4. Ian and Sara, green
> 5. Jack and Jill, yellow

40. SOMETHING TO DO

Clue 1 lists the five boys as Jerry, Larry, the youngest, the oldest, and the one who made a poster. The oldest was assigned to knock down cobwebs (clue 5), and the youngest amused himself by looking at rooms upside down (clue 4). The one who did the jigsaw wasn't the oldest (clue 5) and must have been either Jerry or Larry. Barry isn't the oldest (clue 2), so by clue 1, his recreation was either the poster or he is the youngest who looked at rooms upside down. Therefore, by clue 3, Barry, who didn't empty wastebaskets (clue 2), can only be the one who oiled his skates. He is then not the youngest (clue 4), so he is the one who made the poster. Gary isn't the youngest (clue 4), so he must be the oldest, and the youngest is Harry. Harry didn't empty wastebaskets (clue 3) or wipe the light switches (clue 6), so he brushed the dog. Using clue 3, we know it was Jerry or Larry who did the jigsaw, and we have accounted for Barry's, Gary's, and Harry's chores—so the one who emptied wastebaskets is also Jerry or Larry, and the one who built a model was Gary. By clue 7, Jerry didn't practice foul shots, so Larry must have, while Jerry did the jigsaw. The one who did the jigsaw didn't empty the wastebaskets (clue 3), so Larry did that, and Jerry did the switch plates. In sum:

> Barry: skates, poster
> Gary: cobwebs, model
> Harry: dog, upside down
> Jerry: switches, jigsaw
> Larry: wastebaskets, fouls

41. WEEKEND EXCURSION

One return flight included Sue, Sue's husband, and another of the women (clue 5). Clue 4, then, describes an outgoing flight, since it included Sue, Sam (whose wife was not on the plane), and Mrs. Smith; by clue 3, that flight was via El Paso. The outgoing flight via Phoenix, then, included Sam's wife plus Bob and Ted; one of the latter is Sue's husband, and the other is Mr. Smith. Since Sue's return flight included two women, the other return flight included one woman and two men. This second return flight is the only one of the four that can be described in clue 2, and Mr. and Mrs. Wells were together on this flight. Thus, Sue is not Mrs. Wells and must be Mrs. Dean. The other passenger on the Deans' return flight must have been Mrs. Smith, while Mr. Smith was on the flight with Mr. and Mrs. Wells. Sam, who was with Sue Dean and Mrs. Smith on the outbound flight via El Paso, must be Mr. Wells. Mr. Smith isn't Bob (clue 2), so he is Ted, and Bob is Sue's husband; by clue 3, it was the Deans' flight that returned via Phoenix. Only one of the women, Mrs. Wells, shared her flights with two of the men; she is Ann (clue 1), and Mrs. Smith is Eva. In sum, with the outgoing route listed first:

> Bob Dean: Phoenix, Phoenix
> Sue Dean: El Paso, Phoenix
> Eva Smith: El Paso, Phoenix
> Ted Smith: Phoenix, El Paso
> Ann Wells: Phoenix, El Paso
> Sam Wells: El Paso, El Paso

42. SEE HOW THEY SAT

We are told that men and women alternated around the table, and that no husband and wife sat next to each other. One of the women is Sarah Shepherd (clue 5). Sally sat to the statistician's left and across from Mrs. Stewart (clue 4), so Mr. Stewart must have sat next to Sally; Sally must be the salesperson, and Stephanie sat on the other side of Mr. Stewart (clue 2). Mrs. Stewart's first name must be Susan. Mr. Shepherd sat to her left (clue 8). Sarah Shepherd was not next to her husband, so Stephanie sat to Mr. Shepherd's immediate left, with Sarah Shepherd opposite her. Again by clue 2, Mr. Stewart sat to Stephanie's left and is thus the statistician. Mrs. Sawyer, the ski instructor (clue 1), must be Stephanie, and Sally's last name is Stanton. The man at her left was then not Mr. Stanton and must have been Mr. Sawyer, while Mr. Stanton sat between Susan Stewart and Sarah Shepherd. By clue 6, Mr. Sawyer's first name is then Sam, and Sarah Shepherd is a sociologist. The remaining woman, Susan Stewart, is a songwriter, and Mr. Stewart's first name is Steve (clue 3). Stan can only be Mr. Shepherd, while Sam Sawyer is the stockbroker (clue 7). Sculptor Scott (clue 1) must be Mr. Stanton. Stan Shepherd, by elimination, is a senator. In sum:

Sally Stanton, salesperson
Sam Sawyer, stockbroker
Sarah Shepherd, sociologist
Scott Stanton, sculptor
Susan Stewart, songwriter
Stan Shepherd, senator
Stephanie Sawyer, ski instructor
Steve Stewart, statistician

43. TINY BIRD WATCHERS

All five birds are mentioned in clue 2: Jerry's bird, which was spotted in a walnut tree before the Howell boy's bird, which was seen on a roof and was in turn spotted before the blackbird; the robin, which was spotted before Lenny's bird. The crow seen in an elm tree (clue 3) must have been Lenny's bird, and the pigeon, which wasn't spotted in a tree (clue 4), must have been the Howell boy's. The bird Jerry spotted, by elimination, was the woodpecker. By clue 1, the first bird was spotted pulling a worm out of the ground and the fifth sitting on a fence post; these can only have been, respectively, the robin and the blackbird (clue 2). The crow in the elm tree was spotted by the Caswell boy (clue 5). We know the robin was spotted first and the pigeon was spotted after Jerry's woodpecker (clue 2) and the crow (clue 4), so the pigeon was the fourth bird spotted, and the blackbird was spotted by the Smith boy. The Martin boy didn't spot the robin (clue 6), so the Boswell boy did, and the Martin boy is Jerry; the latter's wasn't the third bird spotted (also clue 6), so it was the second, and Lenny's crow was the third. Johnny's wasn't the first or last (clue 1), so he is the Howell boy. Tony isn't the Boswell boy (clue 7), so Jimmy is, and Tony is the Smith boy. In sum:

1. Jimmy Boswell, robin
2. Jerry Martin, woodpecker
3. Lenny Caswell, crow
4. Johnny Howell, pigeon
5. Tony Smith, blackbird

44. SCHOOL LUNCHES

Remember that each boy ended with a completely different lunch. One boy ended up with a cheese sandwich and a banana (clue 3). A second boy, then, ended up with the ham sandwich and the other piece of fruit, the apple (clue 1). A third boy ended up with a bologna sandwich and a doughnut (clue 5). The fourth boy then ended up with the two remaining items, the peanut butter sandwich and the cupcake. One started with the peanut butter sandwich and the apple and isn't the one who ended up with the cheese sandwich (clue 3), so he can only be the one who ended up with the bologna sandwich and the doughnut. The one who started with the ham sandwich must have brought a banana (clue 1), so he can only be the one who ended up with the peanut butter sandwich and the cupcake. The one who ended up with the cheese sandwich, then, must have brought the bologna sandwich, while the one who brought the cheese sandwich is the one who ended up with the ham. Since we know one ended up with the bologna sandwich and the doughnut, the one who brought the bologna sandwich didn't bring the doughnut (clue 7); he brought the cupcake, and the one who brought the cheese sandwich brought the doughnut. By clue 2, Tony is either the boy who brought the bologna sandwich or the one who ended up with it. The boy who brought the cheese and ended up with the ham isn't Walt (clue 4) or Mike (clue 6), so he is Lew. By clue 2, then, the Archer boy is the one who brought the ham and ended up with peanut butter. The latter is Mike (clue 6), and the one who brought the peanut butter and ended up with the bologna is the Lowe boy (also clue 6). By clue 4, the Lowe boy is Walt, and the one who brought the bologna and ended up with the cheese is the Fry boy. By elimination, Fry's first name is Tony and Lew's last name is McGee. In sum, with the lunch each boy brought and the one he ended up with in that order:

Mike Archer: ham sandwich & banana, peanut butter sandwich & cupcake
Tony Fry: bologna sandwich & cupcake, cheese sandwich & banana
Walt Lowe: peanut butter sandwich & apple, bologna sandwich & doughnut
Lew McGee: cheese sandwich & doughnut, ham sandwich & apple

45.   CENTER CIRCLE FAMILIES

There are only five different numbers which add to fifteen—one, two, three, four, and five; these then, are the numbers of children in the five families. Robert has five children, two girls and three boys, and he is not Mr. Scorps (clue 1). The Scorpses have four children, Lisa and three sons (clue 3). Vickie has two children, a daughter and a son (clue 5). There can be no more than three children whose names begin with the same letter, so Rick and Leslie have three children (clue 2). There are a total of five girls among the fifteen children, and we have thus far accounted for four of them, so Rick and Leslie can have no more than one daughter. Sisters Barb and Laura (clue 6) must be Robert's daughters. Rick and Leslie's children's names, then, all begin with *J;* they are Jill, Jack, and John. Vickie's daughter, by elimination, is Gina. We know the mothers of the two- and three-child families. By clue 4, Gayle must have 5 children and is Robert's wife, Jenny must have 4 and is Mrs. Scorps, and Holly has one child, who must be a boy; Holly isn't Mrs. Vernon. By clue 3, then, Bob is Holly's son and Ron Vernon is Vickie's. By clue 6, since Ben has a son named Sam, he is not married to Holly or Vickie, so he must be Jenny Scorps's husband, and Wayne must be one of Robert and Gayle's children. The Tim Baldwin mentioned in the introduction can only be Wayne's brother. Brothers Scott and Billy (clue 6) must be the remaining Scorps children; the fifth Baldwin child, by elimination, is Luke. Lenny isn't Vickie's husband (clue 5) and must be Holly's. The Webers aren't Rick and Leslie (clue 2), so they are Lenny and Holly. By elimination, Vickie's husband is Brad, and Rick and Leslie are the Cannons. In sum:

> Robert and Gayle Baldwin: Barb, Laura, Luke, Tim, Wayne
> Rick and Leslie Cannon: Jack, Jill, John
> Ben and Jenny Scorps: Billy, Lisa, Sam, Scott
> Brad and Vickie Vernon: Gina, Ron
> Lenny and Holly Weber: Bob

46.   WINTER PAGEANT

Clue 1 lists all five children: the girl who played a fairy, the one who played Hollyberry, the fifth-grader, the one who played a squirrel, and Amy. The child who played Snowflake the bunny is in third or fourth grade (clue 4) and so by clue 1 can only be Amy. Also by clue 4, a girl is younger than Amy and is thus in second or third grade and had no lines (clue 3). Sally had a speaking part (clue 5), and the girl who played the fairy had lines (clue 6), so she was Sally, and the girl younger than Amy is Judy. Fairy Sally's name was not Peppermint (clue 5). Therefore, by clue 4, the children who played Peppermint and the elf must be the two boys. Amy is in third grade, and Judy is in second. By clue 2, Martin is in fourth grade, and the fifth-grader played Candlewick; Sally, the fairy, is not in the fifth grade (clue 1), so the fifth-grader is Joel, and he played Candlewick the elf, while Peppermint was Martin's part. Peppermint must be the squirrel in clue 1. Sally is then in sixth grade, and Judy played Hollyberry. By elimination, Hollyberry was a fawn, and the fairy's name was Starlight. In summary:

> Judy, 2nd: Hollyberry the fawn
> Amy, 3rd: Snowflake the bunny
> Martin, 4th: Peppermint the squirrel
> Joel, 5th: Candlewick the elf
> Sally, 6th: Starlight the fairy

By clue 1, we know Alice was first, the girl in the red T-shirt second, the boy in the blue T-shirt third, the boy in the blue shorts fourth, and George last. By clue 2, one girl and one boy wore a T-shirt in each color listed, and one girl and one boy wore shorts of each color. One girl wore a green T-shirt and yellow shorts, and one wore a yellow T-shirt and green shorts; neither was Alice, and neither was Betty or Jane (clue 3), so they were, in one order or the other, Carol and Kate. The girl in the yellow T-shirt and green shorts, whose partner wore yellow shorts and did not wear a blue T-shirt (clue 6), must have been last, paired with George. He did not wear a green T-shirt, but there was a boy who wore green and yellow, who was not first in line (clue 3); that boy must have worn a yellow T-shirt and green shorts, and he must have been second in line, paired with the girl in the red T-shirt. By clue 4, the only possibility is that the girl in white shorts was the one in the red T-shirt, the boy in white shorts was third in line, and the girl in the white T-shirt was fourth. The girl in the green T-shirt and yellow shorts was then third. By elimination, Alice wore a blue T-shirt and her partner wore red shorts. Since we now know the third girl in line was Carol or Kate, Betty was second (clue 7)—and since we know George's partner was also either Carol or Kate, the girl fourth in line was Jane. Betty's partner in yellow and green wasn't David, Fred (clue 3), or Harry (clue 7); he was Earl. Neither David nor Fred was first in line (clue 3), so Alice's partner was Harry. By clue 8, David can only have been third in line, and his partner was Carol, while Kate was George's partner. Jane's partner, by elimination, was Fred. The girl in red shorts, whose partner wore a red T-shirt, wasn't Harry's partner Alice (clue 5); she was Fred's partner Jane. Since only one boy, Earl, wore green and yellow, George's T-shirt was white, and Harry's was green. Alice's shorts, by elimination, were blue. In sum, with T-shirt color first:

1. Alice (blue, blue) and Harry (green, red)
2. Betty (red, white) and Earl (yellow, green)
3. Carol (green, yellow) and David (blue, white)
4. Jane (white, red) and Fred (red, blue)
5. Kate (yellow, green) and George (white, yellow)

48. RIDE OR HIKE

The Bell boy and Mike were nonhikers and exchanged horses (clue 1). By clue 3, Ringo must have been ridden downhill by Mike Ward, and the Bell boy rode Ringo for the uphill trip. The Rowe brothers both hiked, one to Lookout Hill and the other back to camp (clue 2); Bill hiked uphill with one Rowe boy (clue 4), and Joe hiked down with the other (clue 5). Also by clue 5, Joe rode Star uphill. Greg, who isn't one of the Rowe brothers (clue 4), must be the Bell boy, and the Rowe brothers are Don and Bob. The latter rode downhill (clue 3) while Don is the one who rode up and hiked downhill. The Day boy isn't Bill (clue 4); he is Joe, and Bill's last name is Lee. We know that Mike and Greg exchanged horses, one of which was Ringo. The other two horses were ridden uphill by those who hiked down, and vice versa. The Rowe brothers didn't ride the same horse (clue 2), so Star, ridden by Joe Day, must have been ridden down by Bob Rowe. Greg and Mike didn't ride Molly (clue 6), so Molly was ridden uphill by Don Rowe and downhill by Bill Lee. The horse Mike rode up and Greg rode down, by elimination was Gizmo. In sum, with the mode of travel for the uphill trip listed first:

Greg Bell: Ringo, Gizmo
Joe Day: Star, hiked
Bill Lee: hiked, Molly
Bob Rowe: hiked, Star
Don Rowe: Molly, hiked
Mike Ward: Gizmo, Ringo

49. TRAIN RIDE

Car four was yellow, and at least one of its passengers was a boy (clue 2). Two boys rode in car six (clue 3), and Glen and another boy in car two (clue 6). By clue 5, Laura and the girl who sat with her could only have been in the third car, the second car was green, and Jane rode in the first car. By clue 1, since Danny's car wasn't green, and car six wasn't the blue one (clue 3), he could only have sat in car four, and the fifth car was blue. The white car wasn't car three (clue 4) or car six (clue 3); it was the first car. By clue 8, Mary can only have been in car three with Laura, while Paul rode in car two with Glen—and since Mary's car wasn't red, the red car was car six; Mary's, by elimination, was purple. Andy rode in car one with Jane (clue 1), and the two boys in car six, by elimination, were Bob and Brian. We have now placed all six boys, so two girls rode in car five. Gail rode with her brother Danny (clue 7), so the girls in car five were Eileen and Sue. In sum:

> #1, white: Andy and Jane
> #2, green: Glen and Paul
> #3, purple: Laura and Mary
> #4, yellow: Danny and Gail
> #5, blue: Eileen and Sue
> #6, red: Bob and Brian

50. GEOGRAPHY QUIZ: AFRICA

Since everyone had at least one right and each had a different number right (clue 1), the numbers right were one, two, three, four, and five. Neither the Smith child (clue 3) nor the Roth child (clue 4) got all five right; nor did the Pratt and Tolbert children (clue 5), so the Quill child did. That child is not Edna, who had an even number of right answers (clue 3). From the chart, if the Quill child were Ann, Edna would have only one right. If the Quill child were either Bob or Dave, then Edna and Ann would *both* have two correct answers. The Quill child, therefore, must be Chris. By comparing their answers, we find that Edna had four right; the Smith child had two (clue 3). From the chart, since we know that Chris's answers were all correct, the Smith child is Ann, Dave had three correct answers, and Bob only one. Edna is the Roth child (clue 5). Bob's last name isn't Pratt (clue 2), so it is Tolbert, and Dave is the Pratt child. In sum:

> Chris Quill, 5
> Edna Roth, 4
> Dave Pratt, 3
> Ann Smith, 2
> Bob Tolbert, 1

51. DOGGIE DINNERS

Clues 1 through 4 list all seven dogs' preferences. Spot likes Bowwows, a second dog of the same kind likes Meaty Mix, and each of these dogs is owned by either John or Sam (clue 1). A collie and Chip like Super Snax (clue 2). Boots and Ted's dog both like Crumbles (clue 3), and Rover likes Yappies (clue 4). By clue 4, Blackie must be either the collie that likes Super Snax or Ted's dog; the same is true of Sunny (clue 6). The dog that likes Meaty Mix, then, must be Skeeter. Skeeter isn't Sam's dog (clue 7) and must be John's, while Spot is Sam's dog. Since there are precisely two collies (clue 2), Spot and Skeeter aren't collies. Nor are they spaniels (clue 5), dachshunds, or setters (clue 7); they must be fox terriers. The dogs then include one dachshund and one setter. Since Sam owns Spot, Billy's dog isn't Blackie or Boots (clue 8); Billy's dog isn't Chip or Sunny (clue 9) and must be Rover. Chip isn't a collie, a setter, or a spaniel (clue 2) and must be the dachshund. Sunny is neither the spaniel (clue 5) nor the setter (clue 6) and is therefore one of the two collies; Sunny is then not Ted's dog (clue 3) and must be the collie that likes Super Snax, while Ted's dog is Blackie. Boots is then Ken's dog (clue 4). Charlie isn't Chip's owner (clue 8), so Dave is, and Charlie's dog is Sunny. The spaniel isn't Boots (clue 3) or Billy's dog Rover (clue 5) and must be Blackie. Rover isn't the second collie (clue 2), so Boots is, and Rover is the setter. In sum:

Billy's setter, Rover: Yappies
Charlie's collie, Sunny: Super Snax
Dave's dachshund, Chip: Super Snax
John's fox terrier, Skeeter: Meaty Mix
Ken's collie, Boots: Crumbles
Sam's fox terrier, Spot: Bowwows
Ted's spaniel, Blackie: Crumbles

52. THE BUS RIDERS

None of the ten workers got off the bus at 2nd and Main or at 3rd and Main (clue 2), and all had left the bus before it reached 7th and Capitol (clue 9). Thus, there are six stops at which the ten workers could have gotten off the bus, in order: Main and 4th, Main and 5th, Main and 6th, Main and 7th, 7th and Broad, and 7th and Grand. By clue 3, Edwards was first off the bus, and none of the others got off there or at the next stop. By clue 6, then, Edwards can only have left the bus at Main and 4th, Grey at Main and 6th, French at 7th and Broad, and Jones at 7th and Grand. Davis, who got off the bus before Baker (clue 5), didn't get off at Main and 7th, and Baker didn't get off at 7th and Grand (clue 8), so Davis can only have left the bus at Main and 6th. We now know where five of the ten got off the bus. At least one person must get off the bus at 7th and Main and at least two people have to get off at 7th and Broad (clue 1). If we assume that Baker got off at 7th and Main, and we have already ascertained that French got off at 7th and Broad, there is no way of placing Adams and Carr, or Harris and Innis, who got off the bus in pairs (clue 4), to satisfy clue 1. Therefore, at least two people got off at 7th and Main and, according to clue 1, then four people got off at 7th and Broad. Harris didn't get off before Adams (clue 7), so Adams and Carr got off at 7th and Main. Harris, Innis, and Baker, then all must have exited along with French at 7th and Broad. In sum, in order:

Main and 4th: Edwards
Main and 5th: None
Main and 6th: Davis, Grey
Main and 7th: Adams, Carr
7th and Broad: Baker, French, Harris, Innis
7th and Grand: Jones

53. HOUSEHOLD CHORES

John dusts on Wednesday (clue 5). Mandy is thirteen (clue 6) and washes dishes on Thursday (clue 10). Danny sweeps on Tuesday (clue 11). Either Danny or Mike feeds the cat on Thursday (clue 7), and we know John dusts on Wednesday, so by clue 9, the only possibility is that Jenny washes dishes on Tuesday, feeds the cat on Wednesday, and dusts on Thursday. Either Mike or Danny feeds the cat Friday as well as Thursday (clue 7). The fourteen-year-old who feeds the cat on Tuesday (clue 4) can only be John, while Mandy feeds the cat Monday. Since Jenny feeds the cat on Wednesday, the nine-year-old who empties the garbage on Wednesday (clue 1) is either Danny or Mike. By clue 3, Mike, Mandy, and Danny, in that order, empty the garbage on successive days. Since Mandy does dishes on Thursday and isn't the nine-year-old who empties garbage on Wednesday, those three days must be Monday, Tuesday, and Wednesday, and the nine-year-old is Danny. Jenny empties the garbage on Friday; her Monday chore can then only be sweeping; she is twelve (clue 8). Mike, by elimination, is ten. The day that Danny washes dishes and John sweeps (clue 2), must be Friday—so by clue 7, Mike feeds the cat on Friday and Danny does so Thursday. By elimination, Danny dusts on Monday, while John does the dishes; Mike dusts on Tuesday; John empties garbage on Thursday, when Mike sweeps; Mike does dishes on Wednesday; and Mandy sweeps on Wednesday and dusts on Friday. In sum:

	Monday	Tuesday	Wednesday	Thursday	Friday
Danny, 9	dust	sweep	garbage	cat	dishes
Mike, 10	garbage	dust	dishes	sweep	cat
Jenny, 12	sweep	dishes	cat	dust	garbage
Mandy, 13	cat	garbage	sweep	dishes	dust
John, 14	dishes	cat	dust	garbage	sweep

54. TOO MUCH OF A GOOD THING

We know from the introduction that no two are the same age. Clue 1 tells us Ms. Marcott is two years older than the one who overexercised, who is one year Tracy's senior. Clue 3 also tells us the relative ages of three women: Ms. Wilson is a year older than Mandy, who is two years older than the one who got sunburned. Since there are five women altogether, at least one of those mentioned in this clue is also mentioned in clue 1. Ms. Wilson can't be the one who overexercised (Mandy and Tracy would then be the same age); Mandy can't be Ms. Marcott (the overexerciser and the sunburn victim would be the same age); and the sunburn victim can't be Tracy (Ms. Marcott and Ms. Wilson would be the same age). If Ms. Wilson were Tracy, all five ages would be accounted for, but there would be no way to match up the group described in clue 5 without adding a sixth person. The same reasoning holds true if the oversunner were Ms. Marcott. There is just one possibility: Mandy is the one who overexercised. We then have, in descending order of age, all a year apart: Ms. Marcott; Ms. Wilson; Mandy, who overexercised; Tracy; and the sunburn victim. By clue 5, then, Ms. Wilson is Nikki, Tracy overate, and the oversunner is Ms. Rogers. Tracy isn't Ms. Farrell (clue 1), so Mandy is. She is 22 years old, and Ms. Marcott is Amy (clue 4). Ms. Rogers is then 20, Tracy is 21, Nikki is 23, and Amy is 24. The one who overslept isn't Nikki (clue 2), so she is Amy. By elimination, Nikki spent too much shopping, Ms. Rogers is Shannon, and Tracy's surname is Sukow. In sum:

> Shannon Rogers, 20, oversunned
> Tracy Sukow, 21, overate
> Mandy Farrell, 22, overexercised
> Nikki Wilson, 23, overspent
> Amy Marcott, 24, overslept

55. CAREFREE CRUISING

The five families are named in both clue 3 and clue 5. The Parkers and the Larsens are two of the families; Ned is neither Parker nor Larsen (clues 3, 5), so he represents another family, and since Rose and Sue are not Mrs. Parker or Mrs. Larsen and neither is married to Ned (clues 3, 4, 5), they represent the other two families. Neither Sue (clue 3) nor Rose (clue 4) is the accountant's wife, and neither Ned nor Parker is the accountant (clue 3), so the accountant is Larsen. Neither Sue (clue 4) nor Rose (clue 5) is the doctor's wife, and neither Ned nor Larsen is the doctor (clue 5), so the doctor must be Parker. Thus, by substitution in clues 3 and 5, Rose is from New York, and Sue is from Connecticut. Una does not come from Pennsylvania (clue 1) or Maryland (clue 6), so her home state is New Jersey. Accountant Larsen is not Una's husband, nor is he from Pennsylvania (clue 1), so the Larsens' home is in Maryland. Since Ken is not Una's husband (clue 1), he's not from New Jersey, and he's not Larsen (also clue 1), so he's not from Maryland, or Pennsylvania (clue 1), and is not New Yorker Rose's husband (clue 2), so his home state is Connecticut and his wife must be Sue; he is not the broker (clue 1) or the banker (clue 2), the doctor (clue 4), or the accountant (clue 3), so he is the lawyer. Una's husband is not the broker or accountant Larsen (clue 1) or the banker (clue 6), so he is Doctor Parker; his first name is not Jack (clue 2), or Ned (clue 3), or Mel (clue 6), so it is Lew who is Una Parker's doctor husband. Ned's family, by elimination in clue 3, is from Pennsylvania. Mel is not from Maryland (clue 6), so he is from New York and is Rose's husband; he is not the accountant (clue 3) or the banker (clue 6), so he is the broker; he is not accountant Larsen, or Norris (clue 2) or Miller (clue 6), so he is Olsen. Accountant Larsen from Maryland, by elimination, is Jack; his wife is not Toni (clue 2), so she is Peggy, and Toni's husband is Ned—who is, by elimination, the banker. Toni and Ned are not the Millers (clue 6); they are the Norrises, and Ken and Sue are the Millers. In sum, the five couples, their home states, and each husband's profession are as follows:

> Jack and Peggy Larsen, Maryland—accountant
> Ken and Sue Miller, Connecticut—lawyer
> Ned and Toni Norris, Pennsylvania—banker
> Mel and Rose Olsen, New York—broker
> Lew and Una Parker, New Jersey—doctor

56. ICE DANCING

By clue 1, Jack Peters and his partner wore black and placed first; Ann and her partner wore yellow costumes and placed second; Ms. Kent and her partner placed third; Henry and Ms. Land placed fourth; and Mr. Stark and his partner placed fifth. By clue 5, Ms. Frost and her partner placed eighth; Mr. Nash and his partner placed ninth; and Wayne and Gwen, in gray, placed tenth. Ann's partner wasn't Frank (clue 1), Bob (clue 2), Jim, Mike (clue 4), Bill (clue 6), or Tim (clue 7); he was Tom. By clue 6, then, Ann's last name is Clark; Bill was Ms. Kent's partner, and they wore red; and Mr. Stark's partner was Mary. There is now only one possible place for the sequence described in clue 3: Dee and her partner placed sixth; Mr. Benet and his partner placed seventh; Ms. Frost's first name is Wendy, her partner was Mr. Ulman, and they wore purple. By clue 4, then, Jim can only be Mr. Stark; Mr. Adams was Dee's partner; Mike is Mr. Benet, and he and his partner, Ms. Quinn, wore orange. By clue 2, Dee's last name is Hardin, and Bob was her partner; Jim and Mary wore pink; and Ms. Land and Henry are Diana and Mr. Drake. Mr. Nash's first name is Tim, his partner was Ms. Jacobs, and Wayne and Gwen are Mr. Ryan and Ms. Inness (clue 7). Mr. Ulman, by elimination, is Frank. Bob Adams and Dee Hardin wore neither blue nor white (clue 4); they wore green. Tim and Ms. Jacobs didn't wear blue (clue 7); they wore white, and Henry and Diana wore blue. Ms. Thomas isn't Mary (clue 6) and must have been Jack's partner, while Mary's last name is Ellis. By clue 8, Cathy can only be Ms. Kent and Nancy, Ms. Quinn; Cathy's partner wasn't Olsen (clue 8), so it was Bill McMann, and Tom was Olsen. Gina isn't Ms. Jacobs (clue 5), so she is Ms. Thomas, Ms. Jacobs's first name is Clara. In sum, in winning order:

1. Jack Peters and Gina Thomas, black
2. Tom Olsen and Ann Clark, yellow
3. Bill McMann and Cathy Kent, red
4. Henry Drake and Diana Land, blue
5. Jim Stark and Mary Ellis, pink
6. Bob Adams and Dee Hardin, green
7. Mike Benet and Nancy Quinn, orange
8. Frank Ulman and Wendy Frost, purple
9. Tim Nash and Clara Jacobs, white
10. Wayne Ryan and Gwen Inness, gray

57. LICENSE PLATES AND BARNS

Since everyone saw at least one barn, and one saw only one (clue 7), the numbers of barns seen were one, two, three, four, and five (clue 4). From clues 1 and 4, then, the numbers of license plates seen by the five were two, three, four, five, and six. The boy saw the same number of license plates as barns (clue 9). Since no one saw as many as six barns, by clue 3, the boy must have seen five license plates and Gert two. There were a total of twenty license plates seen, so the parents and the girls together saw fifteen and, by clue 5, the parents together saw eight and the girls seven. The only two of the remaining numbers which add to eight are six and two, so Gert is the mother, the father saw six, one girl saw three, and the other girl saw four. Lee saw two more license plates than one of the girls (clue 8), and Chris saw still more (clue 10), so Lee is the boy, and Chris is the father. The girl who saw four is Lou, and the one who saw three is Kit (clue 6). We know that Lee saw five red barns. A total of fifteen were seen, so the parents and the girls between them saw ten. The girls saw at least six (clue 5), and Kit saw three (clue 6), so Lou must have seen four. Chris saw two and Gert one (clue 2). In sum:

Chris, father: 6 plates, 2 barns
Gert, mother: 2 plates, 1 barn
Kit, girl: 3 plates, 3 barns
Lee, boy: 5 plates, 5 barns
Lou, girl: 4 plates, 4 barns

58.   THE EXIT POLL

Among the five voters, two women's names are mentioned. One voted in the fifth district and lied to the reporter, as did Mr. Bailey, while the second woman and the other two men told the truth (clue 2). By clue 5, the second woman voted in the third district, and Ms. Knox can only be the fifth-district voter, so her statement was false: she actually voted for Perry and no on the bond issue. The other four interviewees, then, approved the bond issue (clue 7), so, by clue 4, Tom's statement was false and he is Mr. Bailey, who voted for Roberts. By clue 3, Ann, who said she voted for Perry, is not Ms. Knox (clues 3, 5) and must be the third-district voter. By elimination, Ms. Knox is Diane. Mr. Greer, who is from either the first or fourth district, said truthfully that he voted for Perry (clue 6), so there were at least three votes for Perry among the five. The first-district voter then voted for Roberts (clue 1), and Mr. Greer is the fourth-district voter. Tom Bailey's district isn't the first (clue 4) and must be the second. Sam isn't from the first district (clue 1), so Mel is, and Sam is Mr. Greer. By clue 3, Mel's last name is West and Ann's, by elimination, is Carson. In sum:

> 1st district, Mel West: Roberts, yes
> 2nd district, Tom Bailey: Roberts, yes
> 3rd district, Ann Carson: Perry, yes
> 4th district, Sam Greer: Perry, yes
> 5th district, Diane Knox: Perry, no

59.   THE SOFTBALL GAME

The introduction tells us that the game consisted of seven innings. In two innings neither team scored (clue 3). Those innings did not include the seventh (clue 1) or the second (clue 7). The score wasn't tied at the end of the second inning (clue 5) but was at the end of the third (clue 4), so at least one team scored in the latter. The score was tied at the end of the fourth inning (clue 4), wasn't at the end of the fifth (clue 8), and was tied again at the end of the sixth (clue 4)—so runs were scored in the fifth and sixth innings. The zero-score innings were then the first and fourth. Since the score at the end of the fourth was 2–2 (clue 4), that was the score at the end of the third, as well. Since the Arrows scored in all five of the scoring innings (clue 6) they scored in the second inning but weren't ahead at the end of the inning (clue 8)—and we know the score wasn't tied at that point, so it must have been 2–1 in favor of the Braves. Since the third inning ended in a 2–2 tie, the Arrows must have gotten one run in that inning and the Braves none, to even the score. We know that neither team scored in the fourth inning. Since both teams scored in four innings (clue 2), both teams scored in the fifth, sixth, and seventh innings. The final score was 8–7 in favor of the Braves (clue 1), so, since the score was 2–2 going into the fifth inning, in the final three innings, the Braves scored a total of six runs and the Arrows a total of five. The Braves scored at least three runs in the seventh inning (clue 1) and at most four (i.e., with one in the fifth and one in the sixth). If we assume four, then the tie score at the end of the sixth inning would have been 4–4. Since the score at the end of the fourth inning was 2–2, and we know both teams scored in both the fifth and sixth innings, that would mean each team had one run in each of those innings, resulting in a 3–3 tie at the end of the fifth inning. But the Arrows led at the end of that inning (clue 8)—so that assumption is wrong, and the Braves must have scored three runs in the seventh inning. The score at the end of the sixth was then 5–5, and the Arrows made two runs in the final inning. That leaves three runs for each team to have scored in the fifth and sixth innings together. Since the Arrows led at the end of the fifth, they scored two runs and the Braves one in that inning, while in the sixth, the Braves scored two and the Arrows one. In sum, with cumulative scores in parentheses:

	1st	2nd	3rd	4th	5th	6th	7th
Arrows	0	1 (1)	1 (2)	0 (2)	2 (4)	1 (5)	2 (7)
Braves	0	2 (2)	0 (2)	0 (2)	1 (3)	2 (5)	3 (8)

By clue 6, Kevin lives in either 105 or 107; by clue 9, Nick lives in either 103 or 107; by clue 3, Mike lives in 103, 105, or 107. So, John and his wife and Larry and his live in 101 and 109, in one order or the other. Neither John nor Larry created "Ye Olde Graveyarde" (clue 8) so that theme wasn't in 109, and Nora doesn't live in 109 (clue 10), so Mike doesn't live at 107 (clue 3). Therefore, we have two possible arrangements: Nick in 103, Mike in 105, and Kevin in 107; or, Mike in 103, Kevin in 105, and Nick in 107. If Nick lives in 103, then, since Mike and Kristi aren't one couple (clue 11), Mike would be Mr. Drake (clue 9). Then by clue 6, since Kevin would be in 107, Mike Drake would have created "Dracula's Castle"—contradicting clue 1. Therefore, the second of the two possible arrangements is correct: Mike resides in 103, Kevin in 105, and Nick in 107. By clues 3 and 8, neither John nor Larry, one of whom lives at 101, created "Ye Olde Graveyarde," so that theme was in 105, and Nora and her husband live in 101. "Ye Olde Graveyarde," in 105, was not created by the Drakes (clue 1), so Kristi is Kevin's wife and the Drakes live in 109 (clue 9). Mr. Drake is not John, so he is Larry (clue 4). John, therefore, lives at 101 and is married to Nora. Linda's husband isn't Larry (clue 2). Since Linda and her husband live next door to the Colemans (clue 5) and Kristi isn't Mrs. Coleman (clue 12), Linda isn't married to Nick; her husband is Mike, and John and Nora are the Colemans. Linda isn't Mrs. English (clue 16), so Mike and Linda's theme was "Dracula's Castle," and Nick is Mr. English (clue 6). The Colemans' theme was not "Invaders" (clue 13), so Mike and Linda are not the Bowers (clue 7), Kevin and Kristi are, and the Englishes' theme was "Invaders from Space" (also clue 7). By elimination, Mike and Linda are the Austins, so the Colemans' theme was "African Safari" (clue 14) and the Drakes' was "The Ghost House." Joan is Mrs. English and Monica, Mrs. Drake (clue 15). In sum:

> 101: John and Nora Coleman, "African Safari"
> 103: Mike and Linda Austin, "Dracula's Castle"
> 105: Kevin and Kristi Bowers, "Ye Olde Graveyarde"
> 107: Nick and Joan English, "Invaders from Space"
> 109: Larry and Monica Drake, "The Ghost House"

61. CAT ANTICS

Of the six cats listed, Pixie is a tawny Abyssinian (clue 1); Scamper is black (clue 3); Grayling is gray (clue 10); Little Bit is white (clue 4); and an orange-and-white cat, which is not Tinker Bell, belongs to Davis (clue 6). There are two black cats, which belong to Helen and Mr. King (clue 1), and one must be Tinker Bell—who, since he doesn't belong to Mr. King (clue 6), is Helen's. Mr. King's black cat must be Scamper. By elimination, Davis's orange-and-white cat is Fuzzy. There are six floors in the apartment building (clue 1). From clue 2, Susan lives on the sixth floor, Larry on the fourth, and Price on the first. From clue 5, the cat that hoards its treasures lives on the sixth floor, Brad lives on the third, and the cat that sleeps on its back on the first. By clue 1, the two black cats live on the same floor, and Pixie and a nonblack cat that dips milk live on another, so the six cat owners live only on these four floors—1, 3, 4, and 6—and there are no more than two cats per floor. Helen isn't Price (clue 2), so she and Mr. King and their black cats must live on either the third or fourth floor. Pixie neither hoards treasures (clue 5) nor sleeps on his back (clue 8), so he and the cat that dips milk don't live on either the first or the sixth floor—i.e., this pair also live on either the third or fourth floor, so Susan's cat hoards and Price's cat sleeps on its back. Pixie lives with a woman (clue 8), who must be Judy, so Price, by elimination, is George. From clue 4, Ms. Blake lives on the fourth floor, the door-top-walking cat on the third floor, and Little Bit is George Price's cat. By clue 7, Adams lives more than one floor below Evans, Evans is Susan on the sixth floor, and, since we know Fuzzy's owner is Davis, Susan's cat is Grayling. The cat that dips milk must be Davis's Fuzzy. Fuzzy isn't Brad's cat (clue 9), so Fuzzy's owner, Davis, must be Larry. Mr. King, Scamper's owner, is then Brad, and Adams is Helen, while Ms. Blake is Judy. Brad King's cat Scamper doesn't walk on the tops of doors (clue 9), so Helen's Tinker Bell does. Nor is Scamper the cat that opens cupboard doors (clue 3), so Pixie is, and Scamper retrieves toy mice. In sum:

6th, Susan Evans: Grayling, hoards treasures
4th, Judy Blake: Pixie, opens cupboards
and
Larry Davis: Fuzzy, dips milk
3rd, Helen Adams: Tinker Bell, walks on doors
and
Brad King: Scamper, retrieves toys
1st, George Price: Little Bit, sleeps on back

62. IMMIGRANT ENTREPRENEURS

By clue 2, the business in Queens and the dress shop opened consecutively in that order. Only two of the five businesses do not involve food. Therefore, by clue 3, the owner of the dress shop is from Poland, and the dry cleaner is in Queens. The first business to open was a restaurant, the last the one in Manhattan (clue 7). The dress shop isn't in Brooklyn, Manhattan (clue 1), or the Bronx (clue 6), so it is on Staten Island; its owner is then Brown (clue 9). By clue 4, the only possibility is that the dry-cleaning business opened second, the dress shop third, and Miller's business fourth, and the fruit stand is in Manhattan. Miller's business, by elimination, is the deli, so he is from Germany (clue 8). Marshall is not the owner of the Manhattan fruit stand (clue 10), so by clue 6, Marshall is the Queens dry cleaner, the restaurant is in the Bronx, and the man from Ireland must own the fruit stand; the deli, by elimination, is in Brooklyn. By clue 5, Allen owns the restaurant, and Marshall is from Italy. By elimination, Allen is from Greece, and Smith owns the fruit stand. In sum, in the order in which the businesses opened:

Allen from Greece: restaurant, Bronx
Marshall from Italy: dry cleaner, Queens
Brown from Poland: dress shop, Staten Island
Miller from Germany: deli, Brooklyn
Smith from Ireland: fruit stand, Manhattan.

63. NEWSPAPER DROPS

Elmwood's population is 1,200, the largest, and another of the towns has a population of 600 (clue 3). Prescott, a third town, has a population of 800 (clue 4); a fourth town, the smallest of the five, has a population of 500 (clue 7). We know that the populations of the five towns are all different. By clue 6, then, the fifth town's population must be 1,000 and is Woodville, while the smallest town was Mike's first stop. The latter isn't Hudson (clue 7), so it is Ellsworth, and Hudson's population is 600. From the introduction, we know that Mike first went to the wrong place in each of the first four towns and was directed to the correct one—and that once he'd dropped newspapers at a correct place, he did not make the mistake of going to that same type of place, since he knew all were different. He also did not repeat any mistakes. When he reached the fifth town, he couldn't make any mistake, since only one type of place remained. Mike went to 4 *wrong* places (clues 1, 2, 4, and 5); in the first, second, third, and fourth towns he visited. In trying to put the businesses in order, you know he had to go to a business in one town by mistake before he could go correctly to that place in a subsequent town. For example, he couldn't have gone to the bakery (who sent him to the hardware store) by mistake before he went to the hardware store by mistake (introduction). So he went to the hardware store by mistake and was correctly sent to the drugstore before he went to the bakery by mistake and was correctly sent to the hardware store. By the same reasoning, he went to the drugstore by mistake before either of these two. You now know the consecutive order of three of the four mistakes. If the cleaner's were his first mistake, this would contradict clue 4—his first stop was Ellsworth and Prescott had the dry-cleaner's mistake. So the dry-cleaner's mistake (in Prescott) had to be the fourth town he visited; the drugstore his first mistake; the hardware his second; the bakery, his third. Since he went to the dry cleaner's by mistake in the fourth town, that must have been the correct stop for the fifth town. The grocery, by elimination, was the right drop in Ellsworth. Woodville was neither the last stop nor the third, where Mike first went to the bakery (clue 6); it must have been the second. The last stop, where the papers were dropped at the dry cleaner's, wasn't Hudson (clue 7), it was Elmwood, the bakery was in Prescott, and Hudson was the third stop. In sum, the drops in order with the mistaken drop listed first and then the correct drop:

1. Ellsworth, pop. 500: drug store, grocery
2. Woodville, pop. 1,000: hardware store, drugstore
3. Hudson, pop. 600: bakery, hardware store
4. Prescott, pop. 800: dry cleaner's, bakery
5. Elmwood, pop. 1,200: dry cleaner's

64.   THE CHEERLEADERS

By clues 1 and 6, the heights range, at one-inch intervals, from 5'2" to 5'6", and the girl with the E is the tallest; the weights are 103, 105, 107, 109, and 111 pounds, and the girl with the F is 103 pounds, the lightest. Lila is the one who weighs 111 pounds (clue 4). From clue 3, Kay weighs 109; the Garner girl, who doesn't have the E, weighs 107; and the girl with the L weighs 105. Since Lila isn't the tallest (clue 4), she doesn't have the E; Kay does and is the tallest at 5'6" (clue 6). By clue 2, the Garner girl must be Mona, the 105-pound girl with the L is the shortest at 5'2" tall, and the 103-pound girl with the F is the North girl. We know the girl with the L is shortest, Kay with the E tallest, so in clue 5, the girl with the I is 5'5", the Fuller girl is 5'4", and Ilene is 5'3". The shortest (5'2") girl at 105 pounds wearing the L is not Lila (111 pounds), Kay (5'6"), Mona Garner (107 pounds) or Ilene (5'3"); she is Judy. Her last name isn't North (clue 2), Murray (clue 4), or Fuller (clue 5); it is Howard. Ilene, at 5'3", can only be the 103-pound North girl. Since Kay is the tallest with the E, Mona Garner is the 5'5" girl who wears the I, and Lila must be the 5'4" Fuller girl (clue 5). By elimination, Lila Fuller wears the D and Kay is Murray. By elimination, the girl with the L is Judy Howard. In sum, in order of weight:

> Ilene North: 5'3", 103 lbs., F
> Judy Howard: 5'2", 105 lbs., L
> Mona Garner: 5'5", 107 lbs., I
> Kay Murray: 5'6", 109 lbs., E
> Lila Fuller: 5'4", 111 lbs., D

65.   WHERE DO THE TREES GO?

By clue 6, the Fosters and the Garners live at diagonally opposite corners of the block, as do the Kayes and the Landmans. The Kayes live on the south side, and not at the east end of the block (clue 5), so they live at #2 and the Landmans at #19. Since the Fosters also live on the south side (clue 1), they live at #20 and the Garners at #1. There was to be no tree in front of the Landmans' home (clue 15), so the trees on the north side were to be planted at #1, #5, #9, #13, and #17. By clue 19, then, those on the south side were to be planted in front of #4, #8, #12, #16, and #20. The families on the north side include the Baers, the Carters, and the Danes (clue 12), so they also include the Hills and the Jacksons (clue 3). The Nivens also live on the north side (clue 14). With the Garners and the Landmans, we now know eight of the ten north-side families. The Ryans, the O'Neills, and the Parkers, who all live on the same side (clue 8), must therefore live on the south side, as do the Elgins (clue 1), the Ingersolls (clue 5), and the Todds (clue 2). Since the Todds live on the south side, the flowering pear was to be planted on the north side (clue 10). The other four trees that were to go on the north side were the beech, the sycamore (clue 1), the linden (clue 8), and the oak (clue 11); all the remaining trees were then to be planted on the south side. The latter included the ailanthus, so the Quinns live on the north side (clue 4). Since the oak was to go on the north side, that is where the Sommers live (clue 11). We now know the names of all the families on the north side, so the Aldens and the Millers must live on the south side. Five houses on each side had no trees and we know that a tree was to be planted in front of the Fosters' home at #20, so none was to be planted at #18. None was to be planted in front of the Kayes' home, since they lived at #2. The Todds' home had no tree either (clues 10, 19), but they cannot live immediately west of the Fosters (clue 7). No tree was to go in front of the Millers' home (clue 18), but the Millers do not live next door to the Fosters either (clue 16). Nor were trees to be planted in front of the O'Neills' and Parkers' homes (clue 8). Since the O'Neills cannot live at #18 (clue 14), the Parkers do. By clue 8, then, the Ryans live at #16 and the O'Neills at #14, and the linden was to be planted in front of #17, directly across from the Parkers' home. Since a tree was to be planted in front of the Nivens' home (clue 10), and they live east of the O'Neills (clue 14), they must live at #17. We have established that there were to be no trees in front of the homes of the Todds and the Millers on the south side, and since the Todds live east of the Millers (clue 7), they live at #10 and the Millers live at #6. The Aldens, then, live at #12. The flowering pear was to be planted at #9 (clue 10). By clue 13, then, the sophora was to be planted at either #12 or #20. But the Landmans live directly opposite #20, so by clue 3, the sophora was to be planted at #12, and the Jacksons live directly across the street at #11. The ailanthus on the south side was to be planted directly opposite the Quinns' house (clue 4). Since the Quinns live east of the Millers at #6 and west of the Ryans at #16 (clue 16), they can only live at #7, and the ailanthus was to be planted at #8. The elm was then to be planted at #4 (clue 18). The beech was to be planted at #13 (clue 4). By clue 17, the sycamore was to be planted at #5 and the ginkgo at #16; by elimination, the oak was to be planted at #1 and the birch at #20. Since the Quinns live at #7 and the Jacksons at #11, the Hills must live at #13 and the Baers at #15 (clue 3). The Carters then live at #9 (clue 18). Since no tree was to be planted in front of the Sommers' home (clue 11), they must live at #3 and the Danes at #5. The family at #4, where the elm was to be planted, must be the Elgins (clue 9); the Ingersolls, by elimination, live at #8. In sum:

> *North side:* #1 Garner (oak), #3 Sommer, #5 Dane (sycamore), #7 Quinn, #9 Carter (flowering pear), #11 Jackson, #13 Hill (beech), #15 Baer, #17 Niven (linden), #19 Landman
> *South side:* #2 Kaye, #4 Elgin (elm), #6 Miller, #8 Ingersoll (ailanthus), #10 Todd, #12 Alden (sophora), #14 O'Neill, #16 Ryan (ginkgo), #18 Parker, #20 Foster (birch)

66.   THE DOUGHNUT SHOP

We are told that each of the six customers bought a different number of doughnuts, and that among them they bought 24 (clue 2). What is the largest quantity any of them could buy, and still leave five different quantities for the others? The least five different numbers can total is 15 (1 + 2 + 3 + 4 + 5 = 15), so the largest order can't be more than nine (24 minus 15). The order for half cinnamon doughnuts and half chocolate doughnuts had to be an even number, and it was also a number divisible by three (clue 3); six is the only such number within the range one to nine, so that customer bought three cinnamon doughnuts and three chocolate. Another half-and-half order was for lemon doughnuts and cinnamon doughnuts in equal quantity; that order was half as large as Mr. Drake's (clue 1). Since Mr. Drake bought twice an even number, he didn't buy six. He bought either 8 or 4. Neither half-and-half order was Ms. Austin's, as she bought three flavors (clue 4). Mr. Ewell bought half as many as Ms. Fox (clue 5); that is, no more than four and, since his order was half of Ms. Fox's, his order could not also be half of Mr. Drake's order. So he did not order either of the half-and-half orders. Ms. Clark bought no lemon, and her order was no larger than four (clue 8). Only Mr. Bond and Ms. Fox, then, could have placed the two half-and-half orders. The all-chocolate order was twice as large as Ms. Clark's (clue 8) and wasn't Mr. Drake's (clue 1) or Ms. Austin's (clue 4), so it must have been Mr. Ewell's. Since his order was even (clue 8), Ms. Fox's order in clue 5 couldn't be the half-and-half order for six, so that must have been Mr. Bond's order, and the cinnamon-lemon order was Ms. Fox's. Mr. Drake's order, then, was double Ms. Fox's (clue 1); hers was double Mr. Ewell's (clue 5); and his was double Ms. Clark's (clue 8). The quantities could only have been eight, four, two, and one respectively. Totaling these four orders and Mr. Bond's order of six, we get 21, leaving just three doughnuts out of the 24 for Ms. Austin's order of three flavors. If she had bought any cinnamon, one of her other flavors would have been either chocolate or lemon, duplicating one of the half-and-half orders, but according to clue 6 no flavor combination was duplicated, so she must have bought one chocolate, one lemon, and one sugar raised. Ms. Clark's one doughnut was then none of these flavors (also clue 6), so it was cinnamon. We know that Mr. Ewell ordered two chocolate doughnuts, Ms. Fox two cinnamon and two lemon, and Mr. Bond three cinnamon and three chocolate. Mr. Clark's eight-doughnut order included no more than four of any one flavor (clue 7), so it must have included more than one flavor. Among the four flavors, there are only six possible combinations: chocolate/lemon, chocolate/sugar raised, lemon/sugar raised (all included in Ms. Austin's order), cinnamon/chocolate (Mr. Bond's order), cinnamon/lemon (Ms. Fox's order), and cinnamon/sugar raised; thus, by clue 6, Mr. Drake can only have ordered the last combination, four of each flavor. In sum:

Ms. Austin: 3 (1 chocolate, 1 lemon, 1 sugar raised)
Mr. Bond: 6 (3 chocolate, 3 cinnamon)
Ms. Clark: 1 cinnamon
Mr. Drake: 8 (4 cinnamon, 4 sugar raised)
Mr. Ewell: 2 chocolate
Ms. Fox: 4 (2 cinnamon, 2 lemon)

67. THE BIG CLEANUP

By clue 5, the five women are Celia, Ms. Bates, Evelyn, Ms. Evans, and Ms. Collins. Since the five first names begin with the letters *A, B, C, D,* and *E,* and so do the five last names, only one of these could have the same first and last initials, Ms. Bates. By clue 7, one does, so Ms. Bates is Brenda, and she cleaned out her kitchen cupboards the first week. Ms. Evans is not Amanda (clue 6), so Ms. Collins is, and Ms. Evans is Doris. Amanda Collins cleaned out her attic the second week (clue 5). None of the women cleaned out her basement the fifth week (clue 4), and no more than two women did the same chore in any one week (clue 1). By clue 5, Evelyn and Doris Evans both cleaned out their basements before Celia, Brenda Bates, and Amanda Collins, so Evelyn and Doris cleaned out the basement the first or second week; Doris cleaned out her garage the first week and her basement the second (clue 8). Ms. Adams also cleaned out her basement the second week (clue 3), so she must be Evelyn. Celia, by elimination, is Ms. Davis. Amanda Collins and Evelyn Adams did the same chores the fourth and fifth weeks (clue 6), and since Amanda cleaned out her basement after Doris and Evelyn, she must have done so the third week. Since Doris Evans cleaned out her garage the first week, Amanda Collins didn't (clue 6); nor did she clean out her kitchen cupboards that week (clue 5), so she cleaned out her closets. By clue 9, she then cleaned out her garage the fourth week (and her kitchen cupboards, by elimination, the fifth week), while Brenda Bates cleaned out her attic the fifth week. Again by clue 6, Evelyn Adams also cleaned out her garage the fourth week and her kitchen cupboards the fifth. Since Evelyn and Doris both cleaned out their basements the second week, Brenda Bates did not (clue 1), so she must have done so the third or fourth week. She and Celia Davis did the same tasks for three consecutive weeks (clue 2); whatever weeks they are, they must include the third week. If they had both cleaned out their basements the third week, when Amanda cleaned out hers, that would contradict clue 1—so Brenda cleaned out her basement the fourth week. Brenda cleaned her kitchen cupboards the first week, and Celia didn't (clue 7)—but both women did that chore before any of the others (clue 5), so Celia must have done so the second week. Brenda and Celia then did identical chores the third, fourth, and fifth weeks—i.e., Celia also cleaned out her basement the fourth week and her attic the fifth week. Doris then did not clean out her attic or her kitchen cupboards the fifth week (clue 1); nor did she clean out her attic the fourth week (clue 4), so she cleaned out her attic the third week, her kitchen cupboards the fourth week, and her closets the fifth week. Brenda didn't clean out her garage the second week (clue 4), so she cleaned out her closets that week and her garage the third week. Celia Davis, as previously established, did the same job as Brenda the third week; so, by elimination, she cleaned out her closets the first week. Since both Amanda and Celia cleaned out their closets the first week, Evelyn didn't (clue 1); she must have cleaned out her attic that week and her closets the third week. In sum:

	1st week	2nd week	3rd week	4th week	5th week
Evelyn Adams	attic	basement	closets	garage	kitchen
Brenda Bates	kitchen	closets	garage	basement	attic
Amanda Collins	closets	attic	basement	garage	kitchen
Celia Davis	closets	kitchen	garage	basement	attic
Doris Evans	garage	basement	attic	kitchen	closets

68. MUDVILLE'S MARCHING BAND

The drummer is a boy who marches in the fourth row (clue 2). The student who marches in the last row isn't Sam (clue 3), Judy (clue 5), Brian (clue 6), Faye (clue 7), Max (clue 9), or Susan (clue 10); he is Tom. Tom doesn't play trumpet (clue 3), trombone (clue 4), flute (clue 7), or saxophone (clue 8); he plays tuba or clarinet. If Tom were the clarinet player, then by clue 9, the

166

Truman girl would march in the fifth row and Max in the sixth. But this leaves no place for the Billings girl, who marches farther back than the fourth row (clue 7). Therefore, Tom plays tuba. The one in the sixth row doesn't play the trumpet (clue 3), flute (clue 7), saxophone (clue 8), or clarinet (clue 9) and must play trombone. Now, by clue 9, the Truman girl, Max, and the clarinet player are in either the first, second, and third row or the third, fourth, and fifth row. If the latter, then the trumpeter and Sam would have to be in the first and second row, respectively (clue 3). The flute player would be in the second or third row, Faye in the fifth, and the Billings girl in the sixth (clue 7). But the trumpet player would then be Brian, contradicting clue 6. Therefore, the Truman girl is in the first row, Max in the second, and the clarinet player in the third. The Truman girl isn't Judy (clue 5) or Faye (clue 7) and must be Susan. Since Sam is immediately behind the trumpet player (clue 3), he is not the boy who plays drums; Brian must be. Sam is either the clarinet player in the third row or the trombonist in the sixth. If Sam were in the third row and the trumpeter in the second, then by clue 7, the flutist would be in the first row. Faye would be in the fifth, and the Billings girl in the sixth. Faye, by elimination, would be the saxophone player. But this contradicts clue 8. Therefore, Sam must be in the sixth row and the trumpeter in the fifth. Tom's last name is Faulkner (clue 3). Now, by clue 7, the flute player is in the first row, Faye in the third, and the Billings girl—by elimination, Judy—in the fifth. Max, by elimination, plays saxophone. Miller, who isn't Brian (clue 6), saxophone player Max, or Sam (clue 8), can only be Faye. By clue 1, Max's last name is Smith and Brian's is Schubert; Sam's, by elimination, is Jilk. In sum:

1. Susan Truman, flute
2. Max Smith, saxophone
3. Faye Miller, clarinet
4. Brian Schubert, drums
5. Judy Billings, trumpet
6. Sam Jilk, trombone
7. Tom Faulkner, tuba

69. ENGLISH AND MATH SCHEDULES

By clues 1 and 2, the class periods involved are 8:00 A.M., 9:00 A.M., 10:00 A.M., 11:00 A.M., 12:00 noon, and 1:00 P.M. By clue 2, each student has English and math—in one order or the other—in consecutive periods, and no two of the five have either English or math at the same time; i.e., in any given period, no more than two of the five can be attending these classes (a maximum of one in English and one in math). There are two women among the five; one and only one of them has these two classes at 8:00 A.M. and 9:00 A.M. (clue 4). By clue 6, Jim and Butler are in class during the same two periods, one in English and one in math during the first, and vice versa during the second. Since none of the five has an English class at 1:00 P.M. (clue 3), those two periods are not 12:00 noon and 1:00 P.M. If Jim's and Butler's classes were at 9:00 and 10:00 A.M., that would mean they would both be in their first class at the same time as the woman who has the 8:00 and 9:00 A.M. classes was in her second class—so that is impossible. If Jim and Butler attended these classes at 11:00 A.M. and noon, there would be no way for the remaining two students to have consecutive classes without three students, being in class at the same time, so that is also impossible. If Jim's and Butler's classes were at 10:00 A.M. and 11:00 A.M., none of the others could be attending these classes at these hours. There could not be two taking the classes at 12:00 noon and 1:00 P.M., since one of those would have to have an English class at 1:00, contradicting clue 3; so just one would have classes at those hours and the fifth student at 8:00 and 9:00 A.M., and the last would be a male. The one with classes at 12:00 and 1:00 could not be Lauren (clue 5), Nick (clue 7), or Michelle (clue 8), so he would be Ken. Michelle isn't Butler (clue 8), so she would be the woman attending classes at 8:00 and 9:00, and Butler could only be Lauren. Jim isn't Dalton (clue 6), so by clue 5, Dalton would be Ken—who would then have math at 12:00 noon and English at 1:00; but that contradicts clue 3, so this assumption, too, is impossible. Jim's and Butler's classes can only be at 8:00 and 9:00 A.M., and Butler is the previously mentioned woman who has classes at those hours; since she is not Michelle (clue 8), she is Lauren. Again by clue 6, Jim isn't Dalton. By clue 5, then, Lauren must have English at 8:00 and math at 9:00 (while Jim's schedule is just the reverse), and Dalton has math at 10:00 A.M. and English at 11:00. By clue 8, Michelle's classes are at 10:00 and 11:00, but she has English before math, so she is a second student who has classes at those hours. According to clue 7, then, Dalton's first name is Nick, and Elliott—by elimination—is Ken. Ken must have classes at 12:00 noon and 1:00 P.M. and, in line with clue 3, he has English at 12:00 and math at 1:00. Michelle is in class at 10:15 A.M., so she is not Abernathy (clue 4); Jim is, and Michelle's last name is Collins. In sum:

Jim Abernathy: 8:00 (math) and 9:00 (Eng.)
Lauren Butler: 8:00 (Eng.) and 9:00 (math)
Michelle Collins: 10:00 (Eng.) and 11:00 (math)
Nick Dalton: 10:00 (math) and 11:00 (Eng.)
Ken Elliott: 12:00 (Eng.) and 1:00 (math)

70. THE AUCTION

By clue 10, at least two bids separated any two bids by the same person. The first three bidders, then, were three different people. Since one bidder, Ian, made a second bid before another bidder, Ms. Davis, made her first (clue 3), Ms. Davis was not one of those first three bidders, and the person who made the first bid also made the fourth. Karen made the eighth bid (clue 4), and the seventh and ninth bids were made by men (clue 13)—by clue 10, two different men. The first bid was $25, the tenth and last $400 (clue 1), and the minimum raise was $25 (clue 12). This means that the fourth bid was at least $100. If Ian were the one who made the first and fourth bids, then, by clue 3, Ms. Davis's first bid would have been the fifth, and it would have been at least $125. Jim would have been either the second or third bidder, and his second bid—the sixth or a subsequent one—would have been at least $150. But this would make Ian's third bid at least $450 (clue 7), more than the final bid of $400. So Ian was not the one who made the first and fourth bids; he made either the second or third bid, and his second bid was the fifth or a later one. It wasn't the sixth, since Ms. Davis's bid followed immediately and we know the seventh was made by a man. If Ian's first two bids were the second or third and the seventh, that would mean the other two early bidders alternated in placing the fourth through sixth bids, contradicting clue 10. Nor can Ian's second bid have been the eighth, since we know he made a third bid—which could then only be the tenth and final bid, which would again contradict clue 10. Ian's second bid, then, can only have been the fifth, and Ms. Davis's entry into the auction was with the sixth bid. Again by clue 10, since Karen made the eighth bid, Ms. Davis must be Linda; the man who made the seventh bid must have been Jim, the one who made the ninth bid Ian; and since Ian made the fifth bid, his first was not the third but the second. We know Linda Davis entered the bidding with the sixth bid, so the third bid was made by either Jim or Karen, and the other of these two was the one who made the first and fourth bids. The third bid was at least $75; if it were Jim's, Jim's second bid would have been at least $300 (clue 9). That would make Ian's third bid at least $900 (clue 7), far in excess of the final bid for the item. Jim was therefore the one who made the first and fourth bids, while the one who made the third bid was Karen. We now know the first nine bids were made, in chronological order, by Jim, Ian, Karen, Jim, Ian, Linda Davis, Jim, Karen, and Ian. The tenth and final bid, by clue 10, was made by either Jim or Linda. If the latter, that would give each woman a total of two bids; but this was not so (clue 6), so the final bid was Jim's. The fourth bid made, which was Jim's second, was $100 (clue 9); given the minimum $25 raise, the second bid (Ian's first) must have been $50, the third (Karen's first) $75. The fifth bid, Ian's second, was $125 (clue 11); the ninth, Ian's third, was $300 (clue 7). Karen's first bid was a $25 raise, so clue 8 must refer to her second, and Case is Jim. The seventh bid, Jim Case's third, was $225 at most; by clue 2, then, Adams can only be Ian, whose first bid was $50, and Jim's third was $200. Linda Davis's only bid was $150 (clue 5). Karen's second bid was $250 (clue 8); her last name, by elimination, is Baker. In sum, the bids in order were:

Jim Case $25
Ian Adams $50
Karen Baker $75
Jim Case $100
Ian Adams $125
Linda Davis $150
Jim Case $200
Karen Baker $250
Ian Adams $300
Jim Case $400

71. ART CLASSES

There are a total of thirty class periods (five days, six periods each day). By clue 11, Ms. Potter teaches two sessions in watercolor, four with the sixth-graders, and three with each of the remaining five grades, for a total of 21 classes. Thus, she has nine free periods during the week. In order for the seven grades to fit into six periods, the watercoloring class must meet in the same period as one of the classes that meets three times a week—i.e., in that period, Ms. Potter has a class every day. By clue 6, that is the third period. We know that she has at least one free period each day. Also by clue 6, she teaches more classes on Wednesday than on other days. If that number were four or fewer, she would have at least fourteen free periods. Therefore, she teaches five periods on Wednesday, with one free period, and she has two free periods on each of the other days. By clue 3, Ms. Potter has Friday's fourth period free, teaches block printing in the fifth period, and teaches the fifth-grade class in the sixth period. On Tuesday, by clue 5, she teaches the second-grade class during the third period, teaches another grade in the second period, and has the first period free; the second-graders aren't doing acrylic painting. The fourth-graders and the class doing acrylic painting both meet on Tuesday, Wednesday, and Thursday only (clue 7), so they cannot be either of those meeting in the fifth and sixth periods, which have Friday sessions; one group must meet in the second period and the other in the fourth. On Monday and Friday, then, Ms. Potter has the second and fourth periods free, so she teaches classes the rest of the day. She has a class in the fifth period on Tuesday (clue 8), her second free period that day is the sixth. The sixth-graders, whose art class meets four times, are not doing block printing (clue 1), so that fifth-period class meets only Monday, Tuesday, and Friday, and Ms. Potter has that period free on Wednesday and Thursday; since she has only one free period on Wednesday, the sixth-period fifth-grade class meets on Wednesday, and Ms. Potter also teaches a class in the first period that day. Since we now know the fifth-grade class meets Monday, Wednesday, and Friday, Ms. Potter has the sixth period free on Thursday and teaches the first period that day. Now, we know that the first-period class meets four times, every day but Tuesday, so that is the sixth-grade class. The weaving class that meets Tuesday, Thursday, and Friday (clue 9) can only be the second-graders, so the twice-a-week watercolor class meets Monday and Wednesday in the third period. By clue 2, the first-graders must meet in the fifth period. The kindergarten class meets on Monday (clue 4) and can only be the third-period watercolor class. The third-graders do not meet in the fourth period (clue 12), so theirs is the second-period class and they must be doing acrylic painting, while the fourth-graders meet in the fourth period. The Tuesday finger-painting class (clue 10) must be in the fourth period. The group doing montages are not the fifth-graders (clue 3), so they are the sixth-graders; the fifth-graders, by elimination, work with clay. In sum:

1st period:	Sixth grade, montages—Mon., Wed., Thurs., Fri.
2nd period:	Third grade, acrylic painting—Tues., Wed., Thurs.
3rd period:	Kindergarten, watercolor—Mon., Wed.
	Second grade, weaving—Tues., Thurs., Fri.
4th period:	Fourth grade, finger painting—Tues., Wed., Thurs.
5th period:	First grade, block printing—Mon. Tues., Fri.
6th period:	Fifth grade, clay—Mon., Wed., Fri.

72. HOUSE PAINT

All the trim colors are listed in clue 4: three red, four white, two blue, and one brown. No two houses have the same basic-color-and-trim combination (clue 4). Basic house colors are: two white (introduction), two yellow and two beige (clue 8), one gray (clue 10), one brown (clue 13), one blue with white trim (clue 6), and one green (clue 5). Eight men are listed, so in addition to the five married couples, there are three single men and two single women. By clue 7, since Paul is the *only* person who lives between two single people, and Peter is the *only* person who lives between two married couples, they must both be single; and precisely three of the five singles, including Paul, live on the north side in adjoining houses, while Peter and the other single live on the south side. Each husband has the same first initial as his wife (clue 3), which leaves Pamela without a partner, so she, too, is single. Mark and Marie are married (clue 6), as are Ken and Karen and Russell and Rosa (clue 12). Ken and Karen used the same trim color as Sam (clue 9) and Russell and Rosa (clue 12). This had to be either white (chosen by four owners) or red (chosen by three). The three single men chose the same trim color (clue 11), and that also had to be either white or red. At least two of those who chose Ken's and Karen's trim color are married,

169

so that color was white, and red was chosen by the single men. Thus, Tom is single (clue 2); therefore, Tanya is the fifth single person, and the other single men, Peter and Paul, also chose red trim. Ned and Nora and Sam and Susan are then the remaining married couples. The single women, Tanya and Pamela, chose the same basic color (clue 11)—i.e., either white, beige, or yellow, each chosen by two owners. The two beige houses are on different sides, and each is directly across the street from one of the two yellow houses (clue 8). Nora and Ned live directly across the street from a house of the same color (clue 12), which has to be white. Thus, Tanya and Pamela chose beige or yellow. Tanya lives on the north side, but she does not have the north-side yellow house (clue 5), so Tanya and Pamela have beige houses, and Pamela lives on the south side. Tom is then the third single person on the north side. Now, by clue 2, Tom can only live at #1 and the Evans couple at #10. From clue 7, Paul lives at #3 and Tanya at #5; since Tanya's house is beige, from clue 8, a yellow house is at #6. We know Peter lives between two married couples—i.e., at #4, #6, or #8—and Pamela does not. If Peter lived at #4, that would leave #8 for Pamela, between married couples. Peter lives at either #6 or #8; in either case, Pamela's house has to be #2, with a married couple in #4. Since Pamela's house is beige, Tom's is yellow (clue 8). Tom's last name is Forrest (clue 5). Ned and Nora live at #4 (clue 9), and we know their house is white, so Paul's last name is Adams, and his red-trimmed house is also white (clue 12). Ned's and Nora's is the white house with blue trim (clue 6), and Pamela's house also has blue trim (clue 9). Tanya must have the beige house with brown trim (clue 4). Now, we know that on the south side, Pamela's beige house is at #2, Ned's and Nora's white house at #4, a yellow house at #6, and the Evans house at #10. By clue 6, the blue house trimmed with white must be #10, Mark's and Marie's house is #6, and Pamela's last name is Carter; Peter's red-trimmed house is then #8. By elimination, #6, #7, and #9 are all trimmed in white. Ken and Karen live directly opposite Russell and Rosa (clue 12) and next door to Sam and Susan (clue 9), so Ken and Karen must live at #9, Russell and Rosa are the Evanses at #10, and Sam and Susan live at #7. Peter is Lyons (clue 1). From clue 10, the Jones house is directly across the street from the gray house, which is next to the Bentley house; the only possible place for the Jones house is at #7, so Peter Lyons's house is gray, and Mark and Marie are the Bentleys. By clue 5, Sam and Susan Jones must have the green house, and Ken and Karen are the DeWitts; the DeWitts' house, by elimination, is brown. Tanya's last name is Harmon (clue 1). By elimination, Ned and Nora are the Grangers. In sum:

North Side
#1: Tom Forrest, yellow with red
#3: Paul Adams, white with red
#5: Tanya Harmon, beige with brown
#7: Sam and Susan Jones, green with white
#9: Ken and Karen DeWitt, brown with white
South Side
#2: Pamela Carter, beige with blue
#4: Ned and Nora Granger, white with blue
#6: Mark and Marie Bentley, yellow with white
#8: Peter Lyons, gray with red
#10: Russell and Rosa Evans, blue with white

73. STUDENTS' ROOMS

From the introduction, the rooms shown, #11 through #14, are all occupied by girls, those directly above them—#21 through #24—by boys; the students in #11, #13, #21, and #23 are all freshmen, the others sophomores; and the students in #11, #12, #21, and #22 are art majors, the other four students math majors. Green is the sophomore math major in #14 (clue 5) so the sophomore art major in #12 is Pat (clue 2). The room farthest from Pat's room is #23; by clue 4, the student in that room is not Black, Silver, Blue, or White. By the same clue, since the room farthest from Green's is #21, the latter isn't Ronnie's; therefore, by clue 2, the student in #23 isn't Brown. The other girl art major, in #11, isn't Silver (clue 3), so the student in #24, the room farthest from #11, isn't Terry (clue 4); by clue 3, then, the student in #23 isn't Gold. The student in #23 can only be Gray. The girl in #13, just below him, is then Lee (clue 1). By clue 4, the student in #21, farthest from Green's, isn't Lou, Terry, Kim, or Ronnie; the student in #22, farthest from Lee's, isn't Silver—so by clue 3, the student in #21 isn't Chris; he can only be Fran. The girl below him, in #11, is White (clue 1). The boy in the room farthest from #11,

170

#24, is then Ronnie (clue 4), so the boy in #22 is Brown (clue 2). Clue 4 mentions all eight students, so the White girl in #11 isn't Lou, Terry, or Kim and must be Chris. The other girl art major, Pat in #12, is then Silver (clue 3). By clue 4, the Gray boy in #23, the room farthest from Pat Silver's, is Terry; the other boy math major, Ronnie in #24, is then Gold (clue 3). Green's first name isn't Lou (clue 5), so Lou can only be the Brown boy in #22; by clue 4, then, Lee in #13, the room farthest from Lou Brown's, must be Black. By elimination, Green's first name is Kim and Fran's last name is Blue. In sum:

> *Girls:*
> #11: Freshman Chris White, art
> #12: Sophomore Pat Silver, art
> #13: Freshman Lee Black, math
> #14: Sophomore Kim Green, math
> *Boys:*
> #21: Freshman Fran Blue, art
> #22: Sophomore Lou Brown, art
> #23: Freshman Terry Gray, math
> #24: Sophomore Ronnie Gold, math

74. THE MYSTERIOUS MURDERS AT MOORHEAD MANSION

The mansion has two stories and the bedroom is on the second floor (introduction). By clue 2, the billiards room, library, and dining room are on the first floor, the conservatory on the second. Mary's portrait was on the first floor, in the east wing of the mansion (clue 1). It was not in the dining room (clue 6), so it hung in either the library or the billiards room. If Mary's portrait were in the library, that would place three portraits in the east wing, with the conservatory directly above, the dining room to the east (clue 2). Since at least two portraits hung in the west wing (clue 4), the billiards room and bedroom would then be in the west wing. The fifth wife's portrait was in the bedroom (introduction), so the first wife's would have been in the billiards room (clue 4). Since Mary and the woman whose portrait hung in the dining room were not consecutive wives (clue 6), they would have been, in one order or the other, Martin's second and fourth wives. By elimination, the portrait in the conservatory would have been of Martin's third wife. By clue 5, Marlena's portrait was not in the dining room, and Marlena was not Martin's fifth wife, so her portrait would have been in either the conservatory (making her the third wife) or the billiards room. If the former, that would place Marianne's portrait in the billiards room, and the portrait in the dining room would be that of Martin's fourth wife (clue 5). The latter would be either Maria or Martha, as would the fifth wife—contradicting clue 3. If Marlena's portrait had been in the billiards room, that, again by clue 5, would place Marianne's in the bedroom. The third wife whose portrait was in the conservatory would be Maria or Martha, as would the second or fourth wife whose portrait hung in the dining room—again, contradicting clue 3. Therefore, Mary's portrait could not have been in the library; it must have hung in the billiards room, which was then on the first floor of the east wing. Returning to clue 2, if the library and the conservatory directly above it were in the east wing, since the dining room is located east of the library, that would place four of the five portraits in the east wing, contradicting clue 4. Thus, the library and conservatory must be in the west wing. Again, by clue 5, Marlena was not Martin's fifth wife, whose portrait hung in the bedroom, nor was her portrait in the dining room. If it hung in the second-floor conservatory, there would be no place for Marianne's portrait, which was on a different floor and west of Marlena's, since we know the dining room is east of the library and the library is directly below the conservatory. The only possibility is that Marlena's portrait hung in the library, and Marianne was Martin's fifth wife whose portrait hung in the bedroom on the second floor west of the conservatory. So, the fifth wife's portrait was in the west wing, as was the first wife's (clue 4). Therefore, Mary was not Martin's first wife; nor was the portrait in the dining room that of Martin's first wife (clue 5). Mary and the woman whose portrait was in the dining room were not consecutive wives (clue 6), so they were, in one order or the other, Martin's second and fourth wives. Maria and Martha, the two we have not yet placed, must have been the two whose portraits hung in the conservatory and the dining room. The one whose portrait was in the conservatory was either the first or third wife—but if she were the third, that would contradict clue 3; so she was Martin's first wife, and Marlena was Martin's third wife. By clue 5, then, the portrait in the dining room was that of Martin's fourth wife, and Mary was Martin's second wife.

Maria's portrait was in the conservatory, and Martha's was in the dining room (clue 3). In sum, with the wives in chronological order:

> Maria, conservatory
> Mary, billiards room
> Marlena, library
> Martha, dining room
> Marianne, bedroom

75. MUSICAL CHAIRS

By clue 8, since only two string instruments—bass and guitar—are mentioned, the six regular band members are: Frank; Janice; Davis, whose primary instrument is the bass; the drummer, whose second instrument is the bass; the regular guitarist; and the one whose second instrument is the guitar. The four standbys, by clue 5, are Ben, Hitchcock, Johnson, and a drummer. The standby keyboardist, who is neither Hitchcock (clue 5) nor Johnson (clue 9), must be Ben. Since Cooper doesn't play clarinet, drums, or trumpet (clue 9), and we know Davis plays bass, and the regular keyboardist sat in for Cooper, Cooper's regular instrument can only be the guitar. So the one whose second instrument is the guitar normally plays the keyboard. The regular trumpeter is then either Frank or Janice, as is the regular clarinetist. Now, by clue 4, Anderson's second instrument is Helen's primary one, and standby Sally plays Anderson's primary instrument. Standby Ben plays the keyboard; standby Sally doesn't play the clarinet (clue 4). She also doesn't stand in for the guitar player since the guitar is Cooper's instrument and Sally fills in for Anderson, so Sally is the standby drummer and Anderson is the regular drummer, whose secondary instrument is the bass. So, Helen is bassist Davis. Paul, a regular band member who does not play guitar (clue 2), must be Anderson. We know that Tom is one of the standbys, as is Diana (clue 1), so George and Ron are both regular band members. One of them plays keyboard, so Iverson cannot be standby keyboardist Ben (clue 7) and must be drummer Sally. If Ron is Cooper, then George would be the regular keyboardist, and his last name would be Fisher (clue 3). Then, by clue 2, Baxter and the clarinetist would be Frank and Janice in one order or the other and the one whose secondary instrument is drums, who could not be Helen Davis (clue 10), would be Ron Cooper. But that contradicts clue 7. Therefore, Cooper's first name is George, and Ron is the regular keyboardist. Now, by clue 7, George is not the one who can fill in on drums, nor is that person Helen Davis (clue 10), or Janice (clue 2); the one whose second instrument is drums must be Frank; Janice is the regular clarinetist, so Frank is the regular trumpeter. Ron must be Baxter (clue 2). Fisher, whose second instrument is the keyboard (clue 3), must be Janice. The clarinet is not George's second instrument (clue 6), so it is Helen's; George Cooper's secondary instrument, by elimination, is the trumpet. We know there is no standby for that instrument, so by clue 1, Diana plays guitar; she is not Hitchcock (clue 5) and must be Johnson. By elimination, Frank's surname is Evans, Hitchcock's first name is Tom, who—since there is no bass standby— plays clarinet; and Ben's surname is Gibbons. In sum:

> *Regulars (primary instrument listed first):*
> Paul Anderson, drums/bass
> Ron Baxter, keyboard/guitar
> George Cooper, guitar/trumpet
> Helen Davis, bass/clarinet
> Frank Evans, trumpet/drums
> Janice Fisher, clarinet/keyboard
> *Standbys:*
> Ben Gibbons, keyboard
> Tom Hitchcock, clarinet
> Sally Iverson, drums
> Diana Johnson, guitar